Interreligious Studies

Other titles from Bloomsbury

Images of Jesus Christ in Islam, Oddbjørn Leirvik
9781441181602

Religious Cohesion in Times of Conflict, Andrew Holden
9781847065360

Muslim World and Politics in Transition, edited by Paul Weller, Ihsan Yilmaz and Greg Barton
9781441120878

Interreligious Studies

A Relational Approach to Religious Activism and the Study of Religion

Oddbjørn Leirvik

BLOOMSBURY
NEW DELHI • LONDON • OXFORD • NEW YORK • SYDNEY

BLOOMSBURY INDIA
Bloomsbury Publishing India Pvt. Ltd
Second Floor, LSC Building No. 4, DDA Complex, Pocket C–6&7,
Vasant Kunj, New Delhi 110070

BLOOMSBURY, Bloomsbury Academic India and the Diana logo are
trademarks of Bloomsbury Publishing Plc

First published in India 2021
First published in 2014

British Library Cataloguing-in-Publication Data
A catalogue record for this book is available from the British Library.

Library of Congress Cataloging-in-Publication Data
A catalog record for this book is available from the Library of Congress

ISBN: 978-93-89351-72-9

For sale in the Indian subcontinent only

Typeset by Newgen Knowledge Works (P) Ltd., Chennai, India

Contents

Acknowledgements

Earlier versions of Chapters 3, 6 and 7 have been published in the journal *Approaching Religion* and in edited books published by Rodopi and Novus Press respectively. They are reprinted here with the kind permission of the publishers. For biographical details, see references in the first endnote to the respective chapters.

I am grateful for inspiration from my colleagues in the European Society for Intercultural Theology and Interreligious Studies (ESITIS), and the research group Interreligious Studies at the Faculty of Theology, University of Oslo.

Introduction: Religious Activism, Interfaith Dialogue and Interreligious Studies

The title of this book includes a number of loaded terms such as 'religion', 'relational approach' and 'activism', as well as the expression 'interreligious'. Explaining my understanding of these terms may be a useful introduction to the book itself.

As claimed by Jonathan Z. Smith in his essay 'Religion, Religions, Religious', *religion* as we think of it today is a modern construct by scholars, a second-order category reflecting the need to organize an ever-expanding knowledge about texts, faiths, rituals and cultural practices: 'The question of "religions" arose in response to an explosion of data' (Smith 2004: 186).

However defined, religion is a chronically unstable category that is often universalized but can only be meaningfully studied with a view to the religions' internal diversity and their perceived relation to religious 'others'. As further explicated by sociologists, religion in its concrete existence must also be understood in relation to other social systems that have been equally differentiated by modernity, such as economy, education and politics (Beyer 2006).

As I will explain in Chapter 1, I see the *relational approach* to the study of religion as a defining feature of 'interreligious studies'. The relational perspective necessitates an awareness of how religions relate not only to each other, but also to internal plurality and – as mentioned above – to other social systems and society at large.

When studying religion and interreligious relations one should also make clear which dimension of religion one focuses upon. With reference to Jonathan Z. Smith's distinction between religion 'Here, There, and Anywhere' (Smith 2004: 323ff.), one might ask: are we referring to the sphere of domestic or family-based religion ('here'), to religion in the civic or national sphere ('there'), or to religious associations and movements that are 'tied to no particular place' ('anywhere')?

There may be a lot of cross-religious activity going on at the everyday level ('here'). However, when we speak of interreligious dialogue the reference is most often to communication of a more official kind. Such ordered communication typically takes place in civil society – be it in a national ('there') or global framework ('anywhere').

The recognition of different levels in the phenomenon of religion also necessitates a critical awareness of who is included or excluded in dialogical enterprises. The cue 'activism' signals a perspective of *agency.* Both confrontational and dialogical movements within the religions reflect conscious decisions – by people who identify themselves as religious – either to defend their identity against perceived enemies, or to engage in trust-building conversations and joint activities. In the latter case, their activism may often be linked to larger networks of action related, for instance, to issues of social justice, gender equality and environmental challenges.

Neither confrontation nor trust-building and joint action comes by itself: it reflects a determination among identifiable actors. As Jeannine Hill Fletcher has noted, an activist perspective on dialogue may also connote a *transformative* interest in bringing about (in the activists' view) necessary changes in religion and society, for instance with regard to gender justice (2013: 174).

As indicated by a book title by David Cheetham, interfaith relations can be studied as multidimensional 'ways of meeting', ranging from the spiritual to the philosophical, from the aesthetic to the ethical (2013). Verbal dialogue constitutes just one modality of such meetings.

Although the present book discusses the modern phenomenon of dialogue between religions, it deals with interfaith or interreligious *relations* in a much broader sense. This includes not just open-minded 'ways of meeting' but hard-nosed clashes as well. In most instances, dialogical initiatives are actually posed as an antidote to more confrontational forms of communication.

With reference to dialogue, the adjectives 'interreligious' and 'interfaith' are often used interchangeably. Inspired by Wilfred Cantwell Smith's famous distinction between reified religion and dynamic faith (1978, first published 1962), one could of course reserve the term 'interfaith' for relationships and dialogues that rely on personal motivation and, to a lesser extent, on institutional representation. The term 'interreligious' would then refer to formalized communication between representatives of the established faith communities, or between the faith communities and the political authorities. But as the expression 'faith community' illustrates, as a common term for institutionalized religion, the distinction between religion and faith is hard to make in light of actual usages. Hence no sharp distinction between these terms will be made in this book.

What are the defining features of dialogue, then, as one out of many modalities of interfaith relations? In its organized forms, interreligious dialogue is a multifaceted phenomenon that nevertheless may be associated with certain characteristics in terms of communication and action. In 2013, a comprehensive 'Companion to Inter-Religious Dialogue' was published, reflecting the fact that 'dialogue' has definitely become a field of academic research (Cornille 2013). Distinguishing dialogue from confrontational or destructive modes of communication, the companion reserves the category of interreligious dialogue for 'any form or degree of constructive engagement between religious traditions' (2013: xii).

The book's two parts deal with 'focal topics' and 'case studies' respectively. The overarching topics range from reflections on the conditions for interreligious dialogue and critical gender perspectives to different modes and aims of dialogue such as scriptural reasoning, comparative theology and social action. The case studies include 17 chapters which are all focused on bilateral dialogue efforts – ranging from Buddhist-Hindu via Christian-Muslim to Confucian-Jewish dialogue.

The companion's case studies illustrate the necessity of a *contextual* approach to dialogue, as a socio-religious phenomenon. Reflecting my own primary field of involvement and research, the main focus of the present book will be on Christian-Muslim relations – in this case, as they evolve in a rather secular environment. The horizon is global and several trends on the international scene, as well as specific national contexts such as Egypt

(Chapter 6), will be addressed. But a good deal of the empirical material (especially in Chapters 2–4) will be taken from the Norwegian context, which is the place from where I speak.

Speaking from a US context, Jane Idleman Smith in her book *Muslims, Christians, and the Challenge of Interfaith Dialogue* (2007) discusses 'Models of Christian-Muslim Dialogue in America'. Smith notes that most Christian-Muslim attempts at overcoming what she calls 'confrontational dialogue' begin – and sometimes end – with a polite 'get to know you' model of dialogue. She then goes on to discuss some more challenging and potentially transformative modalities of interfaith dialogue: the dialogue in the classroom model (cf. my Chapter 6); the theological exchange model (cf. my Chapter 8); the ethical exchange model (cf. my Chapters 3 and 7); dialogical models focused on ritual and spirituality; and, not least, what she terms 'the cooperative model for addressing pragmatic concerns' (Smith 2007: 63–82).

As indicated, most of these models will also be examined in the present book, maybe with the exception of the ritual and spirituality model which – as a separate modality of dialogue – will only be referred to in passing. Although Christian-Buddhist dialogue focused on meditation has been a formative part of my own dialogue experience, my discussion of interfaith dialogue reflects the fact that the main focus of my practice and research has been ethically oriented dialogue between Christians and Muslims. However, both my reflections on Martin Buber's philosophy of dialogue in Chapter 2 and my attempts at a relational theology of religions in Chapter 8 could in fact be read as an exploration of the spirituality of dialogue.

Jane Idleman Smith also offers a power critical perspective on interfaith dialogue, in a chapter titled 'When dialogue goes wrong'. So does Paul Hedges in his book *Controversies in Interreligious Dialogue and the Theology of Religions* (2010). Whereas Hedges highlights how the legacy of colonialism may still persist in 'a continuing cultural imbalance in terms of power relations' (2010: 95), Smith critically focuses on the question of representation ('who speaks for whom?').

With a view to representativity, Smith also notes that real differences tend to criss-cross established cultural and religious barriers. It may thus be 'easier for social and theological conservatives and liberals to talk with their counterparts across religious lines' (Smith 2007: 95). The fact that so many dividing lines – ethical, political, and theological – run right across religious affiliations is also an important recognition underlying my own discussion of interreligious relations.

The present book is not meant as a comprehensive description of different models of dialogue, or other 'ways of meeting'. The aim of the book is to situate and unfold interreligious *studies* as an academic endeavour – marked by relational perspectives both on dialogue and other forms of religious activism.

In the following chapters, I will first situate interreligious studies theoretically as a relational approach to the study of religion (Chapter 1). I will then explore different philosophies of dialogue as they have developed from a 'practice in search of theory' (Chapter 2), before discussing the question of secular language in interreligious dialogue (Chapter 3). In both these chapters, interfaith dialogues in civil society constitute the point of reference for theoretical reflections on religious dialogue in secular environments. In Chapter 4, I discuss the antipodes of interfaith dialogue, focusing on identity politics and 'othering'.

Chapter 5 deals with some political aspects of interreligious relations, discussing *inter alia* the term 'faith-based diplomacy' and the phenomenon of conservative, liberal or radical activism across religious divides. Chapter 6 turns to religious education as a possible arena for interfaith dialogue, in light of globalized concepts such as tolerance, conscience and solidarity, and focusing on current discussions in the Muslim world about how to teach religion and ethics in school. In Chapter 7, the focus will shift from social interaction to the critical encounter between people and texts in a discussion of interreligious hermeneutics and the ethical critique of the scriptures. Chapter 8 is more explicitly theological in its approach, exploring the issue of a relational theology of religions. In Chapter 9, I resume the theoretical discussion of interreligious studies in the academia, in relation to the social phenomenon (or pious aim) of interreligious or interfaith dialogue.

Finally, in a Postscript, I discuss the notion of extremism and religious responses to 'extremist' thought and action.

1

A Relational Approach to the Study of Religion

Interreligious studies . . . What's in a name?

The term 'interreligious studies' is a relative novelty and hard to trace before the late 1990s. Since then, the term has been used to designate an increasing number of chairs, centres, research projects and study programmes in various academic contexts. To cite some examples from the first decades of the new millennium, from different parts of the world: the Claremont School of Theology in California offered an MA in Interreligious Studies and the University of Birmingham, in the United Kingdom, another in Inter-religious Relations. In Yogyakarta, the Indonesian Consortium for Religious Studies – a joint venture of one secular, one Christian, and one Islamic university – offered an international PhD programme in Interreligious Studies.

The University of Oslo has had a chair named 'Interreligious Studies' from 2005. In the same year, a European Society for Intercultural Theology and Interreligious Studies (ESITIS) was formed, thus connecting the well-established notion of intercultural theology with the relatively new one of interreligious studies. As one might expect, in ESITIS 'interreligious' constructs tend to be ever expanding, including for instance the notion of 'interreligious hermeneutics' which was also the title of the Society's biannual conference in 2009.

As an academic discipline, interreligious studies relates to the praxis field of interreligious (or interfaith) dialogue, as reflected for instance in a new chair in 'Comparative Theology and the Hermeneutics of Interreligious Dialogue' established in 2013 at the Free University of Amsterdam. But the scope of interreligious studies is broader, as interfaith relations may just as well mean confrontation and conflict as dialogue and cooperation (diapractice).

As for the notion of interreligious studies, precise attempts to define the term are hard to find. The easiest thing to define is the prefix 'inter', which refers of course to something in between. But between what, or whom? Between texts, traditions or people? The phenomenon of intertextuality is relatively easy to analyse, since we are dealing here with a relation between relatively stable entities; namely texts. When living traditions and people come into the picture, everything becomes more complicated. People cannot be separated into neatly defined religious camps, with a certain 'relation' or 'space' between them. At the level of individual identities, the phenomenon of dual religious belonging (to Christianity and Islam, Buddhism and Christianity, etc.) adds to the complexity.

In pluralistic societies marked by fluidity and constant change, it is hard to see how Christianity, Islam, Buddhism or anything else could ever be fixed as stable points in the landscape, with corresponding spaces in between. Faith as represented by people means a complicated mix of religion, culture and (identity) politics, and the fields of tension are just as often to be found within the religions as between them. A salient example is gender models, as acted out in gendered practices that vary strongly across cultural and religious traditions.

Interreligious or transreligious?

Such recognitions have led some theorists to suggest that the prefix 'inter' should be replaced with 'trans' and that constructs such as 'transreligious' better capture the fluidity and multi-polarity of current religious encounters, and mutual influences across religious boundaries. For instance, in a course description from 2008, Roland Faber defined 'transreligious discourse' as 'an approach to interreligious studies that is interested in processes of transformation between religions with regard to their ways of life, doctrines, and rituals'.[1]

Building on the German theologian Anders Nehring's (2011) critical discussion of the notions of 'intercultural' comparison and encounter, which might seem to imply that cultures are as static entities, the Norwegian theologian Anne Hege Grung suggests that the expressions 'intercultural' and 'interreligious' should be replaced with 'transcultural' and 'transreligious'. In her analysis of a dialogue group of Christian and Muslim women she notes that

> faiths and cultures are in themselves diverse, meaning that transreligious/transcultural encounters are not only happening *across* religious and cultural representations but among different representations of allegedly the *same* religion or culture. (Grung 2011a: 29)

On this basis, she develops two models for dialogue. One (interreligious?) model is based on religious difference as *constitutive*, leaving other differences related to culture, class, gender, etc. more or less in the shadow. The other (transreligious?) model does not treat religions as stable entities. In tune with the analytical perspective of cultural complexity (Hylland Eriksen 2009), other differences related to gender, cultural background, social position and political power are taken seriously as part of the context for religious dialogue. Instead of seeing religious difference as constitutive, a broader array of differences are taken as a *challenge* for dialogue which in this mode may become more power-critical and more open to change (Grung 2011a: 61ff.; cf. Grung 2011b).

At the level of prefixes, there is of course also another distinction to be made; namely that between *inter* and *intra*. The term intercultural (as in intercultural theology) refers conventionally to intra-religious interaction across different cultures, which can be both strenuous and enriching. Anything interreligious is doubly complex, since inter- or trans*religious* encounters are often also inter- or trans*cultural* ones.

Relational studies

In this book, I will stick to the notion of interreligious since the prefix 'inter' – more clearly than 'trans' – points at dynamic encounters that take place *between* people of complex belongings.

Making sense of the term interreligious studies, as a distinct type of approach to the study of religion and theology, requires a clarification of what the intended object of study would be. We could of course say that the object of study is interreligious relations or, more precisely, the encounter between religious cultures, and between people of different faiths. In relation to the well-established field of comparative religion, interreligious studies are 'more expressly focused on the dynamic encounter and engagement between religious traditions and persons' (Hedges 2013: 1077).

But that is not enough to define the academic field. We also need to clarify whether we are dealing with a purely descriptive and analytical study or a more constructive one akin to systematic theology in the Christian tradition.

In my view, there is something essentially relational with interreligious studies that make them different from religious studies in the conventional sense and from confessional theology. In my understanding, the notion of interreligious studies refers both to the *object* of research, and to the *subject* who is carrying out the research (i.e. the researcher and the way in which the research is done). Taking both aspects into account, I would suggest that interreligious studies are *relational* in three different senses: (1) the *object* of study is interreligious relations in the broadest sense, including – I would suggest – the relation between religion and non-religion. Rather than researching one particular tradition, interreligious studies investigates the dynamic encounter between religious (and non-religious) traditions and the space that opens or closes between them. (2) With regard to the *subject* (the researcher) I would contend that interreligious studies are by nature interdisciplinary, as the multidimensionality of interreligious relations can only be grasped by a combination of cultural analytical, legal, social science-, religious studies- and theological approaches.[2] (3) I would also suggest that interreligious studies – at least in the theological sense – can only be meaningfully done *in conversation* between different faith traditions, in an effort at interreligious (i.e. relational) theology.

From a theory of science perspective, interreligious studies can only be meaningfully undertaken in a willingness to reflect critically on one's own position in the spaces between. When studying a separate tradition, it makes sense – to some extent – to state that you yourself need not be implicated yourself in the object of study. Not everyone doing research on Islam is a Muslim and not all those who study Christianity are Christians. But, in the case of interreligious studies, it is hard to see how anyone could say that he or she is not a part of the studied field – especially if we include those complex spaces between religion and secularity that in my understanding are a constitutive part of interreligious studies. Who is not part of the spaces between religions, cultures and secularities? Who is not already a positioned agent in those spaces, when undertaking a particular study? With a view to the many tensions between the religions, and not least between religion and non-religion, interreligious studies thus become studies of conflicts that you are already part of.

If doing interreligious studies means being implicated as an agent in the field of study, it should be no surprise that this emerging field or discipline has evolved from theology rather than from religious studies. Emphasizing the agency perspective, Scott Daniel Dunbar (1998) argues that what he calls 'interfaith studies' in the academia should be experiential and prescriptive, not just descriptive. However, as David Cheetham (2005) has emphasized, the new field needs the critical outsider perspective of religious studies in order not to be controlled by dialogue insiders who are well aware of their role as agents but perhaps not always able to see themselves from a critical distance. In a recent reflection, Paul Hedges suggests that 'interreligious studies' may actually be seen as 'an interface between a more traditionally secular Religious Studies discipline, and a more traditionally confessional theological discipline' (2013: 1077).

Defining features

Summing up and elaborating the above reflections a little more, I see three defining features of interreligious studies as an academic field or discipline:

1. Interreligious studies is something essentially *relational*, in that it focuses on what takes place between religious traditions and their living representatives, on a scale from acute conflict to trustful dialogue. As indicated, my working definition of the space between includes the relation between religion and secularity. Linking up with Charles Taylor's (2007) understanding of the term, secularity itself could in fact be seen as the non-hegemonic condition for interaction between citizens adhering to different religions, confessions and non-religious life philosophies (cf. Chapter 3).
2. Interreligious studies recognizes the researcher's, the teacher's and the student's role as *agents* in the spaces between. Agency means being implicated in negotiations of power, both within the religious traditions and between them. It is hard to see how anyone doing interreligious studies could not be part of this power play. Hence, self-critical reflection on one's

own agency is called for. Actually, the same could be argued with respect to religious studies in the more traditional sense, since the very choice of research objects and perspectives privileges certain strands of a given tradition, and neglects others. Who is not a potential agent of change, then, in the study of religions in today's world?

3 Recognizing one's role as an agent means also to tackle the issue of *normativity* in a transparent way. The normative aspect of the study of religion has to do with the contemporary relevance of religious traditions and how they can be meaningfully translated into new contexts. What makes this work of translation an inter- or transreligious exercise, is the search for meaning and obligation across traditions, through what we conventionally call interreligious dialogue.

As an academic discipline, interreligious studies may investigate the theoretical foundation and practical implementation of different forms of interfaith dialogue. But, just as importantly, interreligious studies – when institutionalized in academia – create another *arena* for dialogue. If based in a secular university, people involved in interreligious dialogue will also have to translate their concerns into a commonly understandable language which includes non-believers in the conversation. In relation to pressing ethical and political issues, normativity is of course just as much a matter of concern for secular-minded colleagues as for religious ones.

With reference to the practice of Scriptural Reasoning, David Ford (2006) has distinguished between conversations in houses, tents and campuses respectively. In addition to the different religions' separate 'houses' of interpretation, 'tents' may occasionally be pitched to frame interreligious conversations about sacred texts and common challenges. In comparison, Ford observes, 'campuses' may offer a more durable and solid structure for interfaith dialogue, if the academy opens up to such activities.

A contextual approach

My reflections above have a particular contextual background; namely, attempts to establish interreligious studies in a particular campus. My campus is the Faculty of Theology, which is a full member of the University of Oslo – a secular state university in the Northern European academic tradition but which also serves the educational needs of the churches (and increasingly, those of other faith communities). In what follows, I will exemplify how interreligious studies is pursued here, in particular, and in other, similar contexts – with reference to (1) ordinary study programmes and courses with an interreligious horizon, (2) tailor-made courses for religious leaders, and (3) the introduction of Islamic theology alongside Christian theology (a development currently seen in many European faculties of theology).

(1) The most common form of interreligious studies, offered by an increasing number of theological faculties and departments of religious studies all over the world, are study *programmes and courses* focusing on interreligious relations. The common recognition behind such courses is that no religion can be studied meaningfully unless in relation to and interaction with other living traditions. A regular course in our faculty, called 'Islam, Christianity and the West', would be a typical example of courses that are largely analytical and descriptive but also includes elements of dialogical reflection. The same would be true of courses that tackle the issue of faith and politics in an interreligious perspective. In other courses, the dialogical and constructive perspective is more outspoken. Examples that could be cited from my faculty include 'Philosophy of dialogue', 'Interreligious hermeneutics' (focusing on joint challenges in biblical and qur'anic interpretation) and a course on 'Jesus, Muhammad and modern identities'. In the last-named course, the questions of the historical Jesus and the historical Muhammad are linked with normative questions about the modern meaning of their messages (as reflected, for instance, in recent biographies, but also in the students' own perceptions). With regard to religion and secularity, students in programmes that include interreligious courses are also required to study humanism and the modern critique of religion.

Some would perhaps ask what makes such courses different from a traditional comparative study. In my view, the difference lies in the orientation towards a *third* element which may constitute a shared challenge. For instance, the above-mentioned course about Jesus and Muhammad has aimed not so much at comparing the two as trying to understand how current understandings of the foundational figures relate to the common question of modern identity. The same reference to a common third could be seen in a course offered by Union Theological Seminary in New York in 2013, about 'Paul and Buddha: Modeling Inter-religious Dialogue'.

Likewise, studying 'Islam, Christianity and the West' means investigating how the two religions respond to shared challenges in contemporary Western societies (including a modern critique of religion).

(2) The second example that could be cited from my faculty is a tailor-made course for religious leaders including imams, pastors, Catholic nuns, Buddhist monks, Sikh leaders, etc. in a continuing education programme about 'Being a religious leader in Norwegian society'. The course has built on the agency of established leaders, with the aim of developing their dialogical competence in a pluralistic society. The modules have dealt with religion, law and human rights; topics such as value pluralism and interreligious dialogue; and the issue of moral and spiritual counselling. My experience indicates that this type of interreligious learning functions as an arena for interfaith dialogue, with much of the same qualities of communication that one conventionally associates with dialogue. Facilitated by the academy as a space between, trust is built, collegiality developed and competence enhanced among religious leaders – many of whom would otherwise not have had the chance to learn together.

(3) Third, some faculties of theology in Europe (including my own) have recently introduced courses in Islamic Theology and Philosophy, taught by Muslim scholars. Several other faculties in Europe have embarked on the same journey, with three universities in the Netherlands (two church-related, one secular) as pioneers (Schepelern Johansen 2006; Drees and van Koningsveld 2008). In Germany, centres for Islamic theology have been established alongside the confessional Protestant and Catholic faculties of theology. In Scandinavia, the situation is different, with less confessional binding of the faculties but, nevertheless, with a rather strong focus on the Protestant-Lutheran tradition. What does it mean to introduce the core subjects of Islamic theology – Qur'an and Hadith studies, Islamic ethics and jurisprudence, Islamic philosophy of religion, Sufism studies, etc. – in such a context? My vision is that the inclusion of Islamic theology will not only make these institutions multireligious faculties of theology but spaces of interreligious learning and dialogue as well. That presupposes that Christian theology and Islamic theology are taught not as parallel options but in academic conversation with each other. In that case, the academy might in fact become the most important arena of long-term and well-founded interreligious dialogue.

Speaking of dialogue about religion and ethics on campuses, religious education in (primary and secondary) school should also be taken into consideration as a potential arena for interreligious learning. This requires, however, religion being taught as an inclusive subject, as is the case in countries such as England, Norway and Sweden. Differently from confessional models for religious education in school in which the aim is 'learning religion', some inclusive models aim not only at 'learning about' religion but also at what could be called 'learning from' religion in a perspective which includes a joint search for meaning and common ethical investigation. Religious education in school may thus not only constitute a mode of its own of interreligious learning, but also an object of interreligious studies (cf. Chapter 6).

My examples and general reflections above are marked by a context with some specific features: a faculty of theology based in a secular university, surrounded by an inclusive subject of religious education in school and – as will be unfolded in the following two chapters – relatively solid structures of interreligious dialogue in civil society. Other contexts may render other emphases and yield other insights. But, in trying to define interreligious studies, one has to take a contextual and bottom-up approach, sharing what is actually taking place within different disciplinary and institutional frameworks and finding out together where that might lead us in a joint effort to define a new field – perhaps even a new scholarly discipline.

My discussion of interreligious studies in the academy will be resumed in Chapter 9.

2

Philosophies of Interreligious Dialogue: Practice in Search of Theory[1]

In late modern philosophies of interreligious dialogue, Martin Buber and Emmanuel Levinas have often figured as important points of reference.[2] The pedagogical and social philosophies of Paolo Freire and Jürgen Habermas are also often cited. None of these – moral, social, pedagogical – philosophers have had interreligious relations as their primary focus in their reflections on dialogue. But their philosophies of dialogue and communicative action have caught the interest of people who have been involved in and/or tried to understand the dynamics of interreligious dialogues. In my case, engagement in philosophies of dialogue has evolved as a practice in search of theory, but also as a search for theory that may enlighten some philosophical aspects of interreligious studies and guide future action in the field of interreligious dialogue.

Spiritual and necessary dialogues

My first reflections on Buber and Levinas can be found in my book about interreligious dialogue in Norway which was published in 1996 (Leirvik 1996: 152–6). At that point, I was in a period of transition from church-based involvement in interfaith dialogue[3] to academic work in the field of interreligious studies.[4] In the book referred to above, I introduced a distinction between 'spiritual' and 'necessary' dialogues (1996: 157–80). Whereas spiritual dialogues are based on personal motivation and guided by an expectation of being enriched by other spiritual traditions (a typical example would be Christians and Buddhists meditating together), necessary dialogues are driven by a felt sociopolitical need to prevent or reduce religion-related conflict in society, by fostering peaceful interaction between representatives of different religious groups.

In what follows, I will distinguish between philosophies of spiritual and necessary dialogues respectively. I will also briefly deal with ethical and religious dialogue in school as a category by itself, under the label of 'dialogue didactics' – a theme that will be further elaborated on in Chapter 6.

As for the notion of necessary dialogue, I shall be referring mainly to interfaith dialogues *in civil society*, initiated by the faith communities. In my Norwegian context, both the bilateral Contact Group between the Church of Norway and the Islamic Council Norway (established in 1993)[5] and the country's multilateral interfaith council (The Council for Religious and Life Stance Communities, established in 1996)[6] have come about on the initiative of the faith communities, with no involvement from the political authorities. It should be noted, however, that in the European context the term 'dialogue' is often used as a heading for *government-initiated communication* with the minority communities, especially the Muslims (Amir-Moazami 2011).[7] In this case, one would expect 'dialogue' to be more oriented towards disciplining measures, in line with Foucault's concept of governmentalization (Lemke 2002) and (more recently) security concerns.[8]

In civil society dialogues, as well, there are imbalances in power. In theorizing about interreligious dialogue, it is still necessary to distinguish between government-initiated 'dialogues' and civil society initiatives – or, in a wider perspective, between dialogue at the levels of state and society respectively. In my following discussion of dialogue (be it 'spiritual' or 'necessary' dialogue), my point of reference will be communication between the faith communities in civil society, not state initiatives.

Philosophies of spiritual dialogue

My first experiences with joint meetings between church and mosque in Oslo took place long before the political authorities had established any form of 'dialogue' with the minorities. It also happened before the increasing politicization of Christian-Muslim relations after the fall of Communism and the First Gulf War. Two of these memorable first events of Christian-Muslim dialogue took place in 1988–9 and was (typically of those innocent times?) focused on the spiritual theme of prayer (Leirvik 1990: 9–18).

Although my main interest as a dialogue activist has been Christian-Muslim dialogue, my work with the Emmaus Centre for Dialogue and Spirituality in the mid-1990s also brought me into conversation with alternative spiritualities. It was in this connection that the philosophies of Buber and Levinas first caught my attention and, in the book from 1996 mentioned above, I engaged both of them in my discussion of the relation between Self and Other in New Age spirituality.

In the same year, Paul Heelas's well-known interpretation of New Age spirituality as 'self religion' was published under the title *New Age Movement. The Celebration of the Self and the Sacralization of Modernity* (1996). In a critical comment to what I saw as a one-sided focus on the Self and a neglect of the relational element of spirituality in many New Age movements, I invoked Buber's remark in *I and Thou*:

> Spirit is not in the I, but between I and Thou. It is not like the blood that circulates in you, but like the air in which you breathe. Man lives in the spirit, if he is able to respond to his Thou. He is able to, if he enters into relation with his whole being. Only in virtue of his power to enter into relation is he able to live in the spirit. (Buber 1987: 57f.)

This was the context for my first encounter with Buber's notion of the space between, which later became a guiding notion also for my reflections on Christian-Muslim dialogue (Leirvik 2006c: Ch. 10 and 26; cf. Illman 2006: 27f.).

Buber's notion of the spirit between was not only formulated as an interpretation of the dynamics of spiritual dialogue but also as a *cultural critique* against any kind of self-centred philosophy. Buber is, however, nuanced in his approach to the question of selfhood and relatedness. Part of the context for Buber's reflections on human relationships in *I and Thou* was Carl Gustav Jung's psychological (and archetypical) perception of Self as distinct from the Ego. In tune with Jung's concern for personal wholeness, Buber valued mystical and psychodynamic practices aimed at 'the soul's becoming a unity' (1987: 112), but only as a preparation for I's authentic encounter with Thou. In this connection, Buber warns also against reducing the notion of dialogue to an internal conversation between I and the (Jungian) Self:

> All modern attempts to interpret this primal reality of dialogue as a relation of the *I* to the Self, or the like – as an event that is contained with the self-sufficient interior life of man – are futile: they take their place in the abysmal history of destruction of reality. (Buber 1987: 111)

These are strong words and the radical nature of Buber's cultural critique as expressed in the above quote can hardly be overlooked. From a metaphysical perspective, Buber was explicitly critical of Jung's insistence that 'the divine action arises from one's own self' (1988: 133). Instead, Buber located also the spiritual (or divine) in what he would later term 'the realm of between' (2002: 243). As he explains in *I and Thou*: 'The extended lines of relations meet in the eternal Thou' (Buber 1987: 57f.).

For me as a Christian theologian, Buber's reflections on the relational nature of human existence and divine reality made deep sense and shed new light on my sometimes frustrated conversations with representatives of New Age spiritualities. In 1996, I supplemented my Buberian critique of self-centred spirituality with insights borrowed from Emmanuel Levinas, whose philosophy at that point I only knew through the Norwegian edition of *Humanisme de l'autre homme* (Levinas 1993) and ongoing research by a friend who applied Levinasian insights on the practice of massage – as a 'dialogue without words' (Grødum 1999).

More clearly than Buber, Levinas emphasized the *difference* between I and Thou – as epitomized by Levinas' substitution of the term 'Thou' for 'the Other'. Whereas Buber's reasoning on the encounter between I and Thou is marked by the intimate language of love, Levinas' meditation on the Other's face is focused on vulnerability and responsibility. In an interview between Levinas and Asbjørn Aarnes (a main proponent of Levinas' thought in Norway), and added to the Norwegian edition of *Humanisme de l'autre homme*, Levinas says (in my translation): 'The wonderful thing about the face is that it speaks; it says: need, vulnerability, it asks, begs *me* for help, it makes me responsible' (1993: 214). This is also how Levinas sees the way to God: 'God, the god, it's a long way there, a road that goes via the Other. Loving God is Loving the Other' (1993: 215, my translation).

By such insights, Levinas strikes a firm bridge from spirituality to ethics and, thus, to the *necessity* of dialogue. In a later edition of my book about interreligious relations in Norway (Leirvik 2001), I returned to Buber and Levinas in a meditation entitled 'God is greater', this time not with reference to alternative spirituality but to religious fundamentalism (2001: 197f.). What I tried to do was to mobilize Buber's critique of reified I-It relationships and Levinas' warning against self-centred attempts to take control of the Other as a critique of both spiritual and political self-sufficiency.

Philosophies of necessary dialogue

When returning to Buber and Levinas in a later book on conflict and dialogue in Muslim-Christian relations (Leirvik 2006c), Buber figures prominently in my use of 'the space between' as a pivotal metaphor – both for interreligious coexistence as a *social* phenomenon and for interfaith dialogue as a *spiritual* practice. At this stage, I also employed the same metaphor to establish a critical research perspective, arguing the impossibility of stepping outside of the space between in order to take a neutral view of social relations in which everyone is already involved (Leirvik 2006c: 113–19, 297–303).

I did not at this stage of my reflection compare Buber's philosophy of between with contemporary social science-oriented notions such as Homi Bhabha's 'third space', which adds valuable insight to the understanding of multicultural interaction. Quite similar to Buber's characterization of the realm between, Bhabha sees the third space in a communicative perspective, when maintaining that production of cultural meaning always transcends the utterances of the I and the You.[9] As Ruth Illman has also noted (2011: 63), Bhabha himself employs the notion of 'inbetween space' when unfolding his concept of the third space:

> [I]t is the 'inter' – the cutting edge of translation and negotiation, the *inbetween* space – that carries the burden of the meaning of culture . . . by exploring this Third Space, we may elude the politics of polarity and emerge as the others of our selves. (Bhabha 2004: 56)

As implied by Bhabha, the third space is not in any way free of contestation. Correspondingly, Michael Barnes in his book *Theology and the Dialogue of*

Religions speaks of a 'negotiation of the middle' (2002: 230ff.) which is 'always broken and always mended' (2002: 250). Whereas Bhabha's approach is that of cultural analysis, Barnes' reflections on the contested middle and Buber's meditations on the realm of between offer a more philosophical contribution to the understanding of social relations and cultural meaning. Buber's philosophy borders on metaphysics, for instance when he speaks of dialogue as a third *dimension* beyond the individual and social aspects of existence:

> In the most powerful moments of dialogic, where in truth 'deep calls unto deep', it becomes unmistakably clear that it is not the wand of the individual or of the social, but of a third which draws the circle round the happening. On the far side of the subjective, on this side of the objective, on the narrow ridge, where I and Thou meet, there is the realm of 'between'. (Buber 2002: 242f.)

Although, at this stage of my reflection process, Buber seemed to be more central to my reasoning than ever, in my book from 2006 I put equal emphasis on Levinas' explicit critique of Buber – particularly as spelled out in his essay on 'Dialogue' in *Of God Who Comes to Mind* (1998) where Levinas emphasizes the asymmetrical nature of human relationships. Suggesting that Buber understands the I-Thou relationship as 'a harmonious co-presence, as an eye to eye', Levinas states: 'There would be an inequality, a dissymmetry, in the Relation, contrary to the "reciprocity" upon which Buber insists, no doubt in error' (1998: 150).

Correspondingly, in his critical dialogue with Buber in *Alterity and Transcendence*, Levinas rhetorically asks: 'The other whom I address – is he not initially the one with whom I stand in the relationship one has with one who is weaker?' (1999: 100). It is in this context that Levinas also speaks paradoxically about 'the distance of proximity' (1999: 93). For him, the expression 'distance of proximity' epitomizes understanding of 'dia-logue' as a form of communication in which one is critically aware of the asymmetry between me and the (almost divine) Other.

Ruth Illman notes that Buber too envisages some sort of dialectic between proximity and distance in human relationships. Even in a close relationship between I and Thou, there will be an element of I-It which maintains an analytical distance and the recognition of irreducible difference (Illman 2006: 26).

What, then, about the allegation that Buber in his interpersonal philosophy presupposes a reciprocity which in Levinas' view reduces the radicality of the ethical demand? In a defence of Buber against Levinas, Andrew Kelly (2004) notes that Buber does not exactly speak of reciprocity but focuses instead on the kind of 'meeting' that characterizes any genuine I-Thou relationship. The central distinction here is that between 'reflecting' and 'addressing'. Whereas reflection takes place in the I and is only related to It, an interpersonal relation presupposes that both I and You are allowed to be as he or she really is, in their otherness: 'It is in this way that speaking – or addressing another – does not destroy the height of the other' (Kelly 2004: 230f.). Something similar, in this line of reasoning, applies to the human being's relation to God, who (in His divine height) can only be addressed in His otherness, not in reciprocity.

In my own practice-related search for theory, I have been interested in finding out why Levinas' insistence on the asymmetry in any social relation (or Buber's notion of being addressed) resonated so strongly with my experience from 'necessary dialogues' between Christians and Muslims in Norway. The first years of the Christian-Muslim Contact Group (from 1993 onwards) were marked by a form of communication in which the Church representatives were addressed (Buber) by their Muslims partners from a moral height (Levinas) – by speaking from below, that is from the perspective of a religious minority searching for recognition in a majority society still heavily influenced by the Christian cultural heritage – and increasingly by secular humanism.

From a more general perspective, it appears that Levinas' emphasis on asymmetrical relationships offered itself as an apt perspective on minority–majority relations, in which the Church of Norway – in spite of the national church's emerging self-understanding as a faith community among others – is inevitably seen as an integral part of majority society. In this sense, the initial distinction I made between dialogue initiatives originating from civil-society actors and the state respectively may be hard to make in practice. For instance, critical research on interfaith dialogue between the faith communities has revealed the extent to which the agenda of such dialogues may reflect the discursive power of the majority representatives (Roald 2002).[10]

In contrast, the multilateral Council for Religious and Life Stance Communities in Norway originated from the minorities' protest against a new compulsory subject of religious education in school, announced in 1995 with a strong priority given to knowledge of Christianity as the country's dominating cultural heritage. As noted, the initial agenda of the Christian-Muslim Contact Group was much focused on Muslim minority concerns in Norway. However, what started out as minority Muslims addressing majority Christians (socially from below, but morally from above) gradually evolved into a form of interaction with clear elements of reciprocity (or mutuality). In my interpretation of Christian-Muslim dialogue in Norway, as I shall demonstrate below, active listening and sensitivity towards the situation of vulnerable minorities has gradually emerged as a *common* practice and *shared* concern. In this process, there is probably both Buberian reciprocity and Levinasian vulnerability and responsibility.

I am referring here not only to the work of the national Contact Group between the Church of Norway and the Islamic Council but also to the work (from 1998 onwards) of the multilateral Oslo Coalition on Freedom of Religion and Belief,[11] in which Christian and Muslim leaders and human rights activists have played important roles in promoting religious freedom and interreligious dialogue with like-minded partners in other parts of the world.

As I have already explained, the early work of the Christian-Muslim Contact Group was marked by attentive listening on the part of the majority church to the minority concerns of Norwegian Muslims. For instance, for Christians, it really took some active listening to understand Muslims' reservations against the new and compulsory subject of religious education in primary and lower secondary schools which (as mentioned) was felt by Muslims, secular humanists and other religious minorities to be dominated by Christian majority interest (a critique that was subscribed to by the European Court on Human Rights in its verdict against Norway in 2007).

Naturally, this contentious issue became a central part of the Christian-Muslim Contact Group's agenda from the mid-nineties onwards. But, at the same time, the Contact Group also engaged itself in the precarious situation of Christian and other religious minorities in Muslim majority societies. Examples of the Contact Group's involvement in such affairs, and the Muslim community's enhanced sensitivity towards Christian minority concerns, can be found in joint declarations, such as the one from 2009 entitled 'Stop the violence against Christians in Pakistan'[12] and in the Islamic Council's swift condemnation and expression of solidarity after the violent attacks against Coptic Christians around Christmas 2010–11.[13] Further aspects of this development will be detailed in Chapter 3.

A possible interpretation of the processes in official Christian-Muslim dialogue in Norway is that the Contact Group has slowly but surely moved towards a joint concern for vulnerable minorities – be it Muslims in Norway or Christians in Pakistan or Egypt. Gradually, a shared concern seems also to have developed for vulnerable individuals whose integrity and well-being may sometimes be threatened by their own cultural and religious group. In some recent statements of the Contact Group, about the right to conversion (2007)[14] and violence in close relationships (2009),[15] the focus of attention has clearly moved from protection of minority *groups* to defence of vulnerable *individuals.* To the extent that such statements are followed up in practice, one may here speak of interreligious dialogue as a form of practical solidarity (Illman 2006: 97).

Dialogue and negotiation

Levinas' focus on asymmetrical relationships, vulnerability and responsibility in dialogue offers itself as an obvious 'theory' of this kind of dialogical practice. But there is also an important element of reciprocity (or mutuality) in these processes, which confirms Buber's view of the dynamics of genuine meeting and dialogue.

However, when Buber exemplifies reciprocity in dialogue, his most striking example has little to do with negotiated 'joint statements' between equal partners. In his essay on 'Dialogue' in *Between Man and Man*, Buber tells a story from Easter 1914 about a broken-off conversation between 'some men from different European peoples [who] had met in an undefined presentiment of the catastrophe, in order to make preparations for an attempt to establish a supra-national authority' (Buber 2002: 6). Buber recalls that one of the Christian representatives considered that too many Jews had been nominated, to which Buber ('obstinate Jew that I am') responded by reminding the Christian that Jesus himself was a Jew. Then in the ensuing heated discussion something strange happens, apparently as a result of the eye-to-eye encounter between these two 'obstinate' men:

> He stood up, I too stood, we looked into the heart of one another's eyes. 'It is gone,' he said, and before everyone we gave one another the kiss of brotherhood. The discussion between Jews and Christians had been transformed into a bond between the Christian and the Jew. In this transformation dialogue was fulfilled. Opinions were gone, in a bodily way the factual took place. (Buber 2002: 7)

The quote illustrates well how far Buber is from an understanding of dialogue restricted to verbally based *negotiations*. In the cited examples from Christian-Muslim dialogue in Norway, there are clearly elements of negotiation, not least in the process towards joint statements on sensitive issues. But, without the personal bonding that takes place over time in serious dialogue, negotiated statements may not be worth much.

Whereas Buber's vision of dialogue is almost mystical and oriented towards the personal bond, other philosophers of dialogue such as Jürgen Habermas seem not to make a clear distinction between dialogue and negotiation. The aim of communicative action in Habermas' sense is exactly negotiated consensus. This is also how he understands the aim of dialogue among religious and secular citizens in his later writings (Habermas 2005). Other theorists of dialogue, however, are keen to distinguish between dialogue and negotiation. In the Norwegian context, Dag Hareide has made a sharp distinction not only between dialogue, debate and discussion, but also between dialogue and negotiation. Whereas negotiation aims at verbally expressed consensus or compromise, says Hareide (2010), dialogue involves the whole person and does not necessarily have agreement as its aim.

In my own experiences from interreligious dialogue, there is something non-verbal and bodily in genuine dialogues, an element which resembles Buber's almost mystical experience in 1914 and indeed Levinas' conception of a 'distance of proximity' in which closeness does not at all presuppose agreement of opinion (verbalized or not). But, as my examples from Christian-Muslim dialogue in Norway illustrate, on the basis of personal trust some sort of negotiation may also take place, in a joint effort to formulate a common stand in critical issues. If and when this happens, it could be for the sake of the vulnerable human being who, in Levinas' sense, should be seen as the invisible *third party* in the encounter between me and the other.

Mutual change

How, then, should the outcome of truly dialogical processes be interpreted? It is interesting to note that in many definitions of dialogue, or even of that which lies beyond dialogue, the notion of mutual change appears as a pivotal one. In 1982, John B. Cobb Jr (whose main horizon is Christian-Buddhist dialogue) published his book *Beyond Dialogue. Toward a Mutual Transformation of Christianity and Buddhism*. The starting point for Cobb's reflections is the radical difference between Christianity and Buddhism which makes it impossible to claim that the two religions actually speak about the same thing. Nevertheless, or exactly because of radical differences, Cobb implies, some kind of mutual transformation may take place in the space between the two religions – provided that Christians and Buddhists (literally) sit long enough together in attentive listening.

Whereas Cobb speaks of mutual transformation as something that takes place *beyond* (verbal) dialogue, the Norwegian dialogue activist and researcher Anne Hege Grung includes the notion of mutual transformation in her very definition of dialogue (or, more precisely, of the potential outcome of dialogue):

> One is not entering a dialogue with the aim of transforming the other(s), but to take part in the possible mutual transformation which might be the result of the encounter. (Grung 2008: 290)

In this perception of dialogue, Levinasian insistence on radical otherness is not sufficient. According to Simone de Beauvoir, insistence on ontological otherness in interpersonal relationships may actually seem to cement stereotyped *cultural* perceptions, for instance of essential differences between the sexes (2010: 8, 757). Levinas' rather one-sided concentration on asymmetry and difference also does not seem to capture the dynamic that evolves when dialogue partners try to live up to the Habermasian ideal of dominion-free communication (Habermas and Kalleberg 1999: 205–11). From a Levinasian perspective, Habermas' communicative vision will always remain a (potentially misleading) ideal. It seems, however, that interreligious dialogue cannot live without this ideal. As expressed by Grung:

> The necessary respect required to start and to continue a dialogue is based on the principle that the partners in the dialogue are equals – equally controlling the themes, the presentation of themselves, the physical circumstances, and the aim of the effort. (Grung 2008: 290)

However, it is exactly in the quest for a jointly controlled agenda that Levinasian insights into asymmetrical relationships are indispensable – in order to have an open and transparent communication about those discursive and political power relations that need to be transformed.

The concept of change in dialogue didactics

I have so far concentrated my reflections on institutionalized, representative dialogues. I have tried to illustrate how impulses from Buber, Levinas and Habermas have interacted in my (and other activist-researchers') quest for theoretical enlightenment of actual practices in these dialogues.

In the Norwegian context, the question of theory and practice in dialogue has also arisen in connection with religious education in school. Having been involved in public debates about religious education and in continuing education of teachers in dialogue didactics, religion in school is part of the field of practice that has triggered my theoretical interest.

Since 1997, Norway is one out of relatively few countries in the world (Sweden and England are two other examples) that have introduced a joint subject of religious education in primary, lower and upper secondary school. As indicated above, the actual subject in primary and lower secondary school has been quite controversial as to its aims and contents. The religious and life-stance minorities have struggled – legally and politically – to change the subject in a more pluralistic and less Christianity-dominated direction and the curriculum has been revised no less than four times in the course of eleven years. After criticism from the UN's Human Rights Committee in 2004 and a verdict against Norway from the European Human Rights Court in 2007, the name of the subject was changed from 'Christianity, Religion and

Life Philosophies' (KRL) to the more neutral 'Religion, Life Philosophies and Ethics' (RLE). The curriculum's revised aim (from 2008) says that religious and ethical education should not only foster 'respect for religious values' but also encourage a 'critical and pluralistic' attitude.

Across these revisions, the aim of creating a common arena for ethical and interfaith dialogue in school remains a central one. The 2008 curriculum speaks of creating space for 'dialogue between people with different views of questions related to faiths and life stances'. It aims at 'dialogue adapted to different age stages'[16] but gives little help to understand how these lofty aims could be translated into didactical practice. It seems also clear that actual teaching practices tend often to be oriented more towards intellectual knowledge than towards existential understanding.

As a contribution to the development of dialogue didactics, in 2003 the Faculty of Theology in Oslo introduced a course with the heading 'Can dialogue be learnt?' which was later transformed into a regular master's course entitled 'Philosophy of dialogue and dialogue didactics'. In this course, the students read recent texts on interreligious dialogue but also the modern classics of Buber, Levinas and Habermas. They also read Nordic and British pedagogues who have sought to translate philosophies of interreligious dialogue into classroom practice, as well as Paolo Freire's dialogical 'pedagogy of the oppressed'.

In Freire's understanding, 'dialogue' is the only form of communication which may free teacher and student from transmission of knowledge similar to bank transactions – thus opening up a space for what Freire calls a 'liberating' pedagogy. This means also that for Freire, true dialogue aims at practice: 'To say the real word – which is work, which is practice – is to change the world' (2003: 62). Here again, the notion of 'change' pops up in connection with philosophies of dialogue, in a conception where self-change can only meaningfully be seen in relation to 'change of the world'.

If one turns to some of the background documents of the school subject KRL/RLE, one will find that both Buber and Habermas (but not Levinas) are important points of references (NOU 1995: 32). Among dialogical values, 'openness and plurality, freedom and tolerance' are cited as examples. Here, too, the dynamic perspective of 'change' is mentioned as a characteristic aspect of dialogical communication – the outcome of which seems implicitly to be thought of as embracement of certain openness values such as those cited above. In a reflection on 'Identity and Dialogue', which is also the title of this background document, it says: 'Whereas identity values emphasize continuity backwards, in relation to our own traditions, dialogue opens up for fresh thinking and change' (NOU 1995: 32). It is also emphasized, however, that change can never be enforced: 'The aim of dialogue is not forcing or alluring or the other to change. That is the hallmark of propaganda. One takes part in dialogue so that *all* may learn, grow and change' (NOU 1995: 32, my translation).

The notion of change can also be found in the first teacher's guide for KRL that was produced in 1997. The teacher's guide notes that dialogue has often been seen as a method of gaining new insight. But if attainment of new insight through dialogue is both possible and legitimate, the guide says, 'one must also be ready to accept that [dialogue] may lead to change – both in oneself and in the partner of conversation'. Probably in view of possible apprehensions among the parents that religious education in school may actually lead to change of religious identity, the teacher's guide adds: 'This [the possibility of change] applies particularly to ethical questions.'[17] Anyhow, a change (religiously or ethically) that may be wanted by some, could be seen as threatening by others (Leirvik 2001: 158).

In the context of the classroom, many pupils will not even have a clear religious identity, which implies that dialogue in the classroom (if it takes place at all) can actually be far more complex – and also more risky – than dialogues among formal representatives of well-defined faith communities. As the controversies around the common subject of religious and ethical education illustrate, it was initially seen by the religious minorities as a majority-defined measure of social integration. If one adds the unequal power relation between teacher and pupil, the question of asymmetry also becomes more acute when talking about dialogue in the classroom. It thus seems that classroom dialogue cannot do without Levinas' critical comments on Buber, since responsible adults must always make sure that a certain 'distance of proximity' is maintained when engaging vulnerable young people in dialogues about religion and ethics.

A critical power perspective

My reflections on philosophies of dialogue are related to dialogue between pupils in the classroom, interfaith dialogue between believers in civil society, and negotiations between the state and the religious minorities. Each of these interactions has their own characteristics and dynamics, and they call for different types of theorizing. But some questions recur across these different arenas of 'dialogue'. Even more than formal conversations between representatives of faith communities, the practice of classroom dialogue illustrates how complex and vulnerable interfaith dialogue may be, and how indispensable a critical power perspective is when reflecting about (mutual?) change as a possible outcome of dialogue.

The power question is probably most acute in state-initiated communication with the minorities. But it would be too simplistic to talk about interreligious dialogue in civil society as a dominion-free activity. Religious education in school illustrates in fact how difficult it is to draw a sharp line between civil society- and state-initiated dialogues. On the one hand, religious education in public school will reflect national ideologies and political priorities, either by giving space to confessional instruction or by opening up an arena for (state initiated) interreligious learning. On the other hand, the school can only contribute to creating good citizens if pupils are also allowed to communicate freely and critically about religion and ethics. In the latter case, dialogue in the classroom may embody some of the same qualities as 'best practices' of civil society dialogues.

3

Interreligious Dialogue and Secularity

In many projects of interfaith dialogue, the language used is distinctively religious – drawing upon the rich resources of faith-based discursive traditions. A fine example of this is the Muslim dialogue initiative from 2007, *A Common Word between Us and You.*[1] The letter known as *A Common Word* was formulated by 138 Muslim scholars and leaders as a conciliatory response to Pope Benedict's unfortunate reference (in a speech in Regensburg in 2006) to a fourteenth-century Byzantine characterization of Muhammad's message as inhuman and violent.

Instead of responding polemically, the Muslims behind *A Common Word* extended an invitation to peace. Addressing church leaders worldwide, and of all confessions, they put forward the double commandment of love – loving God, loving the neighbour – as a uniting bond between Muslims and Christians, conceptually as well as in practical life. The letter elicited a number of Christian responses and involved new groups on both sides in dialogical exchange (Horsfjord 2011). Presenting the letter as a message of peace and understanding, the signatories asserted:

> The basis for this peace and understanding already exists. It is part of the very foundational principles of both faiths: love of the One God, and love of the neighbour. These principles are found over and over again in the sacred texts of Islam and Christianity. The Unity of God, the necessity of love for Him, and the necessity of love of the neighbour is thus the common ground between Islam and Christianity.

Unfolding their invitation, the Muslim signatories quoted extensively from the Qur'an and the Bible. Correspondingly, in the Christian responses (for instance, from archbishop Rowan Williams and a group of scholars and church leaders brought together by Yale University), the language used was replete with theological references.

As for the relation between religious and secular language, *A Common Word* mentions in passing that the second commandment of love can be translated into social principles such as 'justice and freedom of religion'. The letter is also prefaced by a more general outlook: 'If Muslims and Christians are not at peace, the world cannot be at peace . . . The very survival of the world itself is perhaps at stake.'

In the main, however, *A Common Word* and its Christian responses illustrate how Muslim-Christian dialogue may draw on rich scriptural and theological resources when common responses to shared challenges are sought. However, in modern pluralistic societies, debates and dialogues about religion and ethics must also include a critical conversation between religious and secular-minded citizens. Mainly drawing on experiences from the Norwegian context, the present chapter will explore how Christian-Muslim dialogue may also tune in with a 'secular' language. The examples I will be discussing reflect the fact that especially in activist-oriented forms of interreligious dialogue , 'the lines between "sacred" and "secular" are not always clear; religion is always necessarily intertwined with the social and political' (Fletcher 2013: 174).

The issue of 'the secular' is nevertheless a controversial one in interfaith dialogues. The dialogue between believers and non-believers is sometimes more difficult than the conversation between adherents of different religions. Contradictory reality descriptions and mutual suspicion often seem to obscure the communication between religious and secular-minded citizens. Whereas non-believers are wary of religion becoming more visible in the public sphere, religious people fear that mounting secularism will block believers' faith-based engagement in general society. But this is already a simplified description of the state of the debate, as some 'religious' citizens (particularly in the European Protestant tradition) will see secularity and even secularist policies as integral to their non-hegemonic understanding of faith.

In 2008, after a call for new voices in the public debate, the Norwegian liberal-conservative newspaper *Aftenposten* published an award-winning article by the young Muslim medical student Mohammed Usman Rana, titled 'The secular extremism' (2008). The heated debate after Rana's article confirmed that there is much at stake in the issue of religion and secularity. But the debate also demonstrated the necessity of clarifying what we really mean by words like secular, secularity and secularism. Rana himself warned against what he called 'extreme secular' politics, but mentioned also 'the secular model in the U.S.' as a positive example of how constitutional separation of religion and politics may still allow ample space for religious utterances in the public debate.

In this chapter, I will propose a conceptual distinction between secularism and secularity. On this basis, I will discuss whether different forms of religious dialogue can contribute to strengthen what I understand by secularity – by formulating a faith-transcending language for our common life in this world. From a theoretical perspective, I will consider interfaith dialogues' orientation towards a common language in light of John Rawls' and Jürgen Habermas' translation requirements.

Secularization, secularism, secularity

In the public debate there is normally no clear distinction between the notions of secular, secularization, secularity and secularism. Etymologically, every linguistic construct with 'secular' in it goes back to the Latin term *saeculum*. In its ancient origins, the word *saeculum* refers to 'this age' and, hence, to life in this world – as opposed to the 'the last times' and life in the hereafter. In this meaning, the word does not contain any anti-religious connotations. It serves simply to make a temporal distinction between the earthly and the eternal life (Gorski and Altınordu 2008).

When it comes to the concept of secularism, sociologists Gorski and Altınordu note a development from the *temporal* connotations of the word *saeculum* (as, for example, used by Augustine) to the *spatial* associations connected with the later word *saecularizatio*. For instance, in medieval (Catholic) Canon Law 'secularization' was used with a spatial reference to monks who walked out of the monastic community (Gorski and Altınordu 2008: 60).

The third layer of meaning was, according to Gorski and Altınordu, established during the Reformation, when the term 'secularization' was used about the Protestant sovereigns taking over church properties. Secularization in the modern meaning of the word (the fourth layer of meaning in the taxonomy of Gorski and Altınordu) is only found in nineteenth-century Western Europe, in connection with a political programme that secularized key social institutions by freeing them from priestly power and the grip of the churches.

From then on, it also makes sense to talk about 'secularism' as a political project aimed at establishing a sharp distinction between religious and political powers. Inspired by Enlightenment legacy, political secularism is often linked to a more general critique of religion on moral or rational grounds.

By virtue of this conceptual history, 'secularization' today includes both political projects and religion-critical attitudes. In general parlance, 'secularization' has moved from being a political programme to signifying a more general, societal process that makes religion less visible in public places, with a corresponding decline in religious attendance.

In this way, the term 'secularization' has gradually acquired a reasonably clear meaning, as a reference to social processes with specific characteristics. Like other 'isms', 'secularism' connotes, to a greater extent than secularization, a political programme. What then of 'secularity'? What does it stand for, as opposed to secularism?

My impression is that one rarely makes a sharp distinction between secularism and secularity. Charles Taylor is among those who prefer the adjective 'secular' and the noun 'secularity' over against 'secularism'. In *A Secular Age* (2007) he distinguishes between three forms of secularity, with reference to (1) secular public space, (2) general decline in religious practice, and (3) modernity's 'conditions of belief' which implies a critical awareness that one's own belief is only one possible choice among many others (Taylor 2007: 1–3, 15).[2]

By blending the notion of 'secularity' with elements of what others would refer to as 'secularism' or 'secularization', Taylor hardly contributes to more clarity as regards the difference between these three terms. The most interesting aspect of secularity, which Taylor himself emphasizes, is the common awareness that one's own belief is only one out of many possible convictions and that it neither has a general endorsement nor is in a position to make any claim for hegemony.

In the following, I will take 'secularity' as a reference to a common, non-hegemonic condition in pluralist societies. At this level, secularity functions as a descriptive category, although the non-hegemonic condition referred to may often seem to oscillate between analytical description and normative prescription. The normative aspect of secularity, as I understand it, becomes even more visible when (as I will be doing) speaking of secularity as a common language.

Secularity as a common space – for dialogue

In accordance with the conceptual distinctions above, 'secularization' refers to a social *process*, 'secularism' to a political *programme* (in the spectrum from hard to soft secularism), and 'secularity' to a cultural *precondition* (in line with Taylor's 'third secularity').

Taylor's third secularity – understood as a shared sociocultural condition – can actually be seen as a starting point for the late modern phenomenon of interreligious dialogue. Behind the will to dialogue there is not only an acceptance of the pluralistic condition but also the recognition that faith-based convictions may just as well lead to conflict enhancement as to open dialogue. Interreligious dialogue (also in the framework of religious education in school) could thus be seen as a way to counteract faith-based entrenchment and belief-related fragmentation of society. In other words, the necessity of interreligious dialogue can only be realized in opposition to the globalized phenomenon of religious identity politics (cf. Chapter 4).

The term interreligious dialogue has its conceptual history. Searches in media archives show that in the Norwegian context, the word 'religionsdialog' was first used in any significant scale from the mid-1990s and with a sharp increase after 2000.[3] Interreligious dialogue may either refer to an informal conversation between people of different faiths or to more institutionalized communication between faith communities. As indicated in the previous chapter, the various forms of interreligious dialogue can either be oriented towards spiritual sharing or develop as a political virtue of necessity.

The basis for 'necessary' dialogue is that people of different faiths realize that some sort of confidence-building, perhaps also consensus-seeking, conversation about urgent ethical and political questions has to take place in the public sphere in order to foster constructive coexistence.

From this perspective, secularity can be seen as a way of living together in which no religion or spiritual authority has the hegemony but must share power and influence with other movements, institutions, and lines of thought. Regardless of how strong religion is considered to be in a given society, this is the secular condition.

In this understanding, secularity is akin to Habermas' ideal type of dominion-free (not religion-free) spaces of communication in society. Interreligious dialogue could then be seen as a way to fill 'the spaces between' with meaningful, confidence-building and conflict-resolving conversation.

Does interreligious dialogue strengthen or weaken the established religions?

In his aforementioned article from 2008, Mohammed Usman Rana accused secular extremism of marginalizing religion and religiously committed people by pushing them out of the public debate. But to many secular-minded citizens, his article gave the (obviously frightening) impression that it is now the religions, with Islam in the lead, that are on the offensive – ready to challenge the secular foundations of society.

In the dominant discursive order, however, it is the religions that have to defend themselves in the media by responding to the often well-founded complaints about authoritarian and anti-modern attitudes that collide frontally with the dominant values in secular society. Despite this sense of being pressurized by secular society, can religions still embrace the secular, non-hegemonic condition as defined above?

Asking such questions, one has often the individual religion in mind. Can Christianity – in its various confessional varieties – embrace modern secularity? Can Islam accept it?

If the question is formulated in this way, it might seem that the religions are brought before a (presumed neutral?) secular court. Another, more open-ended way to pose the question would be to ask what happens when representatives of various religions – normally, on their own initiative – engage each other in conversation. Do such dialogues strengthen the religions and their position in society, or do they entail relativism, perhaps even a weakening of religions?

These two questions – whether interreligious dialogue strengthens or weakens the religions' position in society – correspond to fairly common concerns about interreligious dialogue from, respectively, secular-liberal and religious-conservative quarters.

When the national Contact Group between the Church of Norway and the Islamic Council of Norway was announced in 1992, several conservative Christians were worried that a formalized dialogue between Christians and Muslims in Norway would lead to an unfortunate mixing of religions and a general relativization of their truth claims.[4] On the other hand there were those who foresaw that the fresh contact initiative would join Muslims and Christians in a common front against racism, homosexual partnerships and alcohol consumption.[5] To those who – with positive or negative expectation – foresaw a value-conservative, Christian-Muslim alliance, an official church representative responded that the contact initiative aimed at establishing 'common conversation, not a common front'.[6] With regard to conservative expectations, these were not really met by the new Christian-Muslim forum, which (as noted in Chapter 2) developed rather a vulnerability-oriented and human rights-based approach to dialogue.

When the Christian-Muslim Contact Group was established in 1992–3, the event was barely registered by the general public. Hence no liberals seemed to be intimidated by the prediction of a value-conservative alliance between Christians and Muslims. From 1993 onwards, interreligious dialogue in Norway (as in many other countries) has increasingly been institutionalized – in bilateral forums such as the Christian-Muslim Contact Group, the multilateral Council for Religious and Life Stance Communities (from 1996) and the more internationally oriented Oslo Coalition on Freedom of Religion or Belief (from 1998).

With reference to the 1990s and the first years of the new millennium, it is fair to say that the little interest that was dedicated to interreligious dialogue by the general public, was, in the main, positive. As interreligious dialogue has grown stronger, however, popular attitudes to the dialogue movement have become noticeably more negative among secular-minded citizens and particularly among Islam-critical bloggers.[7] The controversy over the Danish

Mohammad-caricatures in 2005–6 seems in many ways to have been a turning point (Leirvik 2006b, 2011c). During the cartoon controversy Norwegian authorities, in their attempts to find conciliatory solutions to the conflict, leaned heavily on the established structures for interreligious dialogue. For instance, representatives of both the government and the opposition presided over a public reconciliation between the Islamic Council and the editor of the newspaper (*Magazinet*, a mouthpiece of the New Christian Right) which had republished the Danish cartoons as a warning against Islam as 'a religion that is not alien to resorting to violence'.[8] The Foreign Ministry also funded Muslim-Christian delegations to the Middle East and Pakistan in order to demonstrate Norway's alleged dialogical approach to the controversy – an approach particularly articulated by Foreign Minister Jonas Gahr Støre.[9] The ensuing debate demonstrated that some people felt that this ostentatious promotion of the culture of dialogue was simply too much of a good thing, serving only to circumscribe tough and necessary debates about religion, violence and freedom of expression.[10]

The critique of institutionalized dialogue between religions is based partly on a perception that interreligious dialogue by its very nature shuns conflict,[11] and partly on a fear that dialogue – when religious leaders join hands – may reverse the secularization process and give the established religions more power. Some self-proclaimed secular Muslims also argue that interfaith dialogue only serves to strengthen the religious institutions and their position in society.[12]

Understandably, secular liberals will be particularly critical if Christians and Muslims work together to promote conservative positions, as when in 2005 Christian and Muslim leaders in Kristiansand (a city located in the Norwegian Bible belt) actually formulated a joint petition against plans that had been announced to introduce a gender-neutral marriage act.[13] The mentioned op-ed by Mohammed Usman Rana – with its overt appeal to value-conservative Christians – could also be read as an invitation to form such interfaith alliances.

The conservative concern about interreligious dialogue is the exact opposite to the liberal fear that it will strengthen the religions' political position. Many conservatives seem to fear that interfaith dialogue will lead to a watering down of religions, since one's own position may be relativized in an open conversation with others, which (according to conservative apprehensions as well as many theorists of interreligious dialogue) may entail unforeseeable change. In an article titled 'Softening in inter-faith discourse' (2003), the Swedish theologian Kajsa Ahlstrand reflects on the potentially softening aspects of true dialogue. Her point is that dialogue over time may lead to a change of attitudes that implies less concern about demarcations and confrontations, and more acceptance of real existing plurality. Theologically, a close encounter with people who think differently may also lead to a recognition that religious diversity is actually willed by God.

From a social science perspective, the same process could be seen as the formation of an 'ethic of civility', which (according to James Davison Hunter) implies that conservative believers who engage themselves in local community work or national politics may, over time, become more tolerant of others' beliefs but also more 'tolerable to others' in the sense that intolerant, religious absolutism tends to be underplayed in faithful interaction with citizens of other convictions (Hunter 1987: 182–5).

From Ahlstrand's perspective, the aforementioned Christian-Muslim petition against a gender-neutral marriage act was not exactly an expression of open-ended, interreligious dialogue. The petition represents, rather, a pragmatic alliance based on certain conservative-value convictions that can be recognized across the borders of faith. Internationally – not least in the UN system – the last few decades have witnessed many examples of this type of alliance between conservative Christians and conservative Muslims, particularly in issues related to so-called family values, such as opposition to feminist legal reforms, abortion and legalization of gay marriage (Butler 2006). But as a Christian American lobbyist said some years ago, commenting on such attempts at Christian-Muslim alliances: We are allies, but not necessarily friends.[14]

Secularity as a common language

What are the characteristics of religious dialogue, then, as distinct from more pragmatic types of cooperation between religions? As noted in Chapter 2, theorists of interreligious dialogue often point to 'the possible mutual transformation which might be the result of the encounter' (Grung 2008: 290). Change can happen with regard to relationships (one may become friends, not merely allies) but has also to do with attitudes in controversial questions. My experience from interfaith dialogue in Norway (I am referring here to institutionalized dialogues, where the results of dialogue are actually quite identifiable) is that serious conversation over time has changed the religious leadership's attitudes on critical issues. As indicated in Chapter 2, there is evidence that the dialogue between Christian and Muslim leaders in Norway has united the parties in a common concern for religious minorities and their situation – whether related to the plights of the Muslim minority in Norway or the worsening situation for Christians in Pakistan (and other Muslim majority societies).

But which minorities may enjoy joint Christian-Muslim concern? A common concern for sexual minorities is obviously more difficult to develop than a shared commitment to religious minorities. Perhaps, over time, a more general concern for vulnerable minorities will develop, in tune with the hate-speech paragraph in the Norwegian penal code (§ 135a) which protects sexual minorities on a par with ethnic and religious ones.

A common defence of vulnerable minorities may be expressed in a traditionally religious language. However, when Christians, Muslims and other religious citizens – as a result of the dialogue – arrive at a common attitude on certain issues, it will often be expressed in a common language which – in accordance with my definitions above – may be termed as secular. Being focused on common human values rather than on special religious interests, interreligious declarations often lean more on human rights-inspired language than on specifically religious resources.

Maybe one can go so far as to characterize this as a *systemic* feature of interreligious dialogue, namely, that it reaches out for a common language which – in line with the word *saeculum*'s reference to our common life in this world – may well be characterized as secular. But in which sense is this a necessary process? With reference to organized Christian-Muslim dialogue in Norway, it might seem to be a simple description of processes that have actually taken place. It might still be that the actors in question have consciously, and on a normative basis, chosen to embrace the secular condition and its requirement for a common language.

From a contextual perspective, there may also be something in the Lutheran tradition of the Northern European countries that points in the same direction.

As Roger Jensen points out in an article about 'Secular reason vs. religious feelings' (2008), the Lutheran tradition is bent on translating religious values into a common language, in tune with Luther's understanding of the human being's secular calling. Many forms of religious dialogue seem to pull in the same direction: dialogue articulates not particularistic, religious discourses but a search for commonly binding language. And when religious discourses are activated through dialogue, the goal is normally 'to work one's way to common parameters for thinking about humanity and society' (Jensen 2008: 92).

In this way, I will argue, interreligious dialogue regularly meets Jürgen Habermas' translation requirement for communication in the public sphere – in that religions and secular world views alike try to translate their concerns into language in which a public conversation can be performed (2005). Even though Habermas' requirement of translation is primarily directed towards political and legal decision-making processes in society, it can also be seen as a civil ideal of a much broader range, including the entire political communication within society:

> The truth content of religious contributions can enter into the *institutionalized* practice of deliberation and decision-making only if the necessary translation already occurs in the pre-parliamentarian domain, i.e., in the political public sphere itself. (Habermas 2005: 15)

But is this a matter of translation, or have human rights language and other tropes associated with 'common ethics' already become an integrated part of many believers' reasoning, at least in the Northern European perspective? Apart from the Protestant reference above, Cora Alexa Døving, in her chapter about Norwegian hijab debates in a book about secularism through Norwegian lenses, notices that young Muslim women tend to argue their right to wear the hijab not with reference to religious demands but to human rights principles and matters of individual choice (2012).

To the extent that these discourses nevertheless contain an element of translation, Habermas' translation requirement (which is addressed to secular citizens as much as to religious ones) comes close to the ideal that John Rawls sets up when he speaks of 'public reason' and 'the duty of civility'. Even though Rawls has mainly the representatives of the government and the judiciary in mind, he too underlines that ordinary citizens also have a moral and political obligation to explain their beliefs in a language than everyone can understand

('... explain to other citizens their reasons for supporting fundamental political positions in terms of the political conception of justice they regard as the most reasonable', 1997: 769).

In Rawls' terminology, 'public reason' differs from 'secular reason'. Rawls sees secular reason as an expression of a 'comprehensive doctrine' (i.e. secular humanism) which, just as much as religious belief, requires explanation and translation to a more general language. It is this common language that I (as distinct from Rawls) would call secular, as it seeks to articulate our common humanity and our obligations in a common life-world.

My use of the term secularity also differs from Habermas' notion of the post-secular society. If secularity refers to a common language in a common world, secularity is not something that has to be modified or transcended in order to accommodate religious beliefs in public spaces. Secularity is, on the contrary, the social condition for the common language which interreligious dialogue almost regularly reaches out for.

A pre-modern, Islamic perspective on common language

Before I give some concrete examples of how Norwegian interfaith dialogue has drawn in the direction of a common, secular language, I will mention a pre-modern role model for interreligious conversations that have common values and common humanity as their horizon. The example may also serve to illustrate the point I have made that religious people do not necessarily have to 'learn' a secular language from sources outside their own tradition. It may already be there, at least as a historical potential.

I am referring here to the intensive cooperation between Muslims and Christians in Baghdad and surrounding regions in the ninth and tenth centuries, when Muslims and Christians – in a joint intellectual effort sponsored by the Caliph – translated a vast part of the Greek philosophical heritage, including the works of Plato and Aristotle, into Arabic. In this way they articulated not just one but two common languages: a Greek language of mind and the written language of Arabic.

Why did they make this common effort? One of their aims was to write works about virtue ethics in a philosophical language that transcended the borders of faith and articulated a common humanity. For instance, the main works of the Muslim philosopher Miskawayh (d. 1030) and his Christian mentor Yahya ibn 'Adi (d. 974) carry the same Greek-inspired title: 'Refinement of the human character'. Earlier in the tenth century, al-Farabi wrote a work entitled 'The virtuous city', which on Platonic and Aristotelian models articulated a common political ethics.

Linguistically, it is in this era that Arabic coins a separate word for 'humanity'; namely *insaniyya*. Humanity was the common horizon of these philosophers, not Muslim or Christian group interest (Leirvik 2002: 122–42). In the words of Miskawayh: 'To this end people must love one another, for each one finds his own perfection in someone else, and the happiness of the latter is incomplete without the former' (Miskawayh 1968: 14).

It was not (unfortunately, some would say) humanistic philosophy or its theological relative Mu'tazilism that became the dominant line of thought within classical Islam. But the legacy is strong enough to serve as an inspiration for dialogue-minded Muslims and Christians today. It is well known that the humanistic philosophy from this era has also – through a several-centuries-long detour via Spain and Ibn Rushd to Thomas Aquinas – helped to save the Greek humanist inheritance for Europe.

From a critical perspective, we must of course recognize that Greek philosophy is just as little 'common' as any religious language. I would still argue that the humanistic, Muslim-Christian project in the Middle East in the ninth and tenth centuries (and later in Spain) had much the same essential features as when Christians and Muslims today are approaching each other in a common, human rights-inspired language. In our time it is not the Greek classics but modern human rights thought and (I would add) the ethics of vulnerability that provide dialogue-oriented Christians and Muslims with a common frame of reference. But the horizon is the same; namely the common humanity.

A humanistic, human rights-inspired language

In the discussion about religion and human rights it is often, with reference to John Rawls and other political philosophers, claimed that the various religions and life stances (on the basis of their respective 'comprehensive doctrines') must be able to meet in an overlapping consensus on universal human rights.[15] They can. But maybe this is about more profound processes than what is reflected in a superficial consensus. My experience from interreligious dialogue is that human rights language not only offers itself as a secondary common language but that human rights thought (by virtue of its orientation towards common humanity) also helps to *transform* the religions in a process that the social anthropologist Tordis Borchgrevink has tentatively called 'globalizing secularity' (2004).

For example, what starts with a religious minority's invocation of human rights in pure self-interest may, in the long term, mean that you are being caught by the inner logic of the human rights discourse – so that you gradually develop a more principled endorsement of such fundamental principles as non-discrimination of other beliefs, protection of all vulnerable minorities and an inclusive understanding of citizenship. Such processes can be seen in both the Muslim minorities in the West and in the Christian minorities in Muslim majority societies. In some groups, the application of human rights language may still be the expression of a purely strategic choice, unless it leads to more profound changes with regard to universal standards.

How has interreligious dialogue in Norway helped to shape a common language that is secular – not in the sense of non-religious, but universally understandable and commonly binding?

There is one particular element of the Norwegian dialogue scene that may have influenced what we might term the humanistic turn in interfaith dialogue. I am referring here to the central role that the Nansen Academy – known as the Norwegian Humanistic Academy – played in the first institutionalized dialogues in the 1990s. The headings of the dialogue projects that took place at the Nansen Academy were – tellingly enough of their 'secular' orientation – 'Community Ethics in a multicultural Norway' (Eidsvåg and Leirvik 1993) and 'Religion, Life Stances and Human Rights in Norway' (Eidsvåg and Larsen 1997). It is also worth noting that the Humanist Association from the outset has been an active participant in what should, therefore, more accurately be called 'religious and ethical conversation' in Norway. The secular humanists' participation has not lessened the challenge to find a common language. But this is a challenge that the faith communities have embraced, not least through the Council for Religious and Life Stance Communities which from 1996 has been the broadest forum for religious and ethical conversation in Norway.

But also in the bilateral Contact Group between the Church of Norway and the Islamic Council which was established in 1993, can a similar orientation towards a common human rights language be identified. Christian-Muslim dialogue in Norway has for a great part had social coexistence as the focus of the conversation (more than theological themes). Tellingly, the first joint statement of the Contact Group (from 1994) carried the headline 'A common space for ethics and religion in school'. Then came the contentious KRL-subject mentioned in Chapter 2 and the ensuing conflicts about religious education in school. Notably, these conflicts did not block the conversation but, rather, opened up for a clearer understanding of both the minorities' concern about (Lutheran) Christianity's dominant position in public institutions, and the need for common learning about religion and ethics in school.

The difficult conversations about religious education in various forums for interreligious dialogue has clearly made the Church of Norway – referred to in the constitution as the National Church of Norway ('Norges Folkekirke') – more understanding of the Muslims' and other minorities' scepticism about being forcibly integrated in a subject that they (especially in the first phase) saw as too influenced by Christian majority interest to be genuinely inclusive. After the legal struggle to make the subject more inclusive, the question now is whether everyone can accept that religious education in school can actually be part of the *saeculum*, which means that the focus should be on the children's and the young people's common life-world, rather than on the self-interest of the religions and the life-stance communities. If that succeeds, religious education in school might also strengthen secularity – not in a way that weakens the religions but by opening a common space where young citizens can be trained in developing a common language for conversation about religion and ethics.

In the question of state and church, the Church of Norway's open dialogue with Muslims and other religious and life-stance minorities has clearly helped to sharpen the human rights profile of the Church's social ethics. When a Church-initiated report about future relations between state and church ('Same church, new arrangements', 2002) so emphasized the principle of non-discrimination, it is reasonable to see this as a ripe fruit of the Church's obligating interfaith and ecumenical dialogue.

As the Church of Norway has become slightly less power arrogant in the public sphere and more sensitive to minorities, it has simultaneously raised the critical issue of Christian minorities in the Muslim world. Already in the mid-1990s, the difficult situation of the Christian minority in Pakistan hit the table of the Contact Group. The background was three death sentences against Christians (one of them a minor), based on the country's draconic blasphemy paragraph in Pakistan's Penal Code that allows for capital punishment for defamation of the Prophet. The paragraph is regularly used as a pretext for fabricated accusations against religious minorities (Ahmadiyya Muslims, Shi'ites, Christians) in Pakistan. Since it had been revealed that some Muslim leaders in Norway supported the death sentences, this also became a difficult case within the Christian-Muslim dialogue in Norway.

In 1995, there was some frustration on the Christian side that the Islamic Council did not take a clear-cut stance in this case. Even if the Council problematized the actual sentences in several ways, a more principled rejection of the possibility of sentencing people to death for such alleged offences was not clearly expressed. Since then, many Muslim leaders in Norway have developed a more fundamental endorsement of human rights principles and, on this basis, joined hands with other believers (and atheists) in an interreligious commitment to minority protection.

One manifestation of this joint commitment is the so-called Oslo Coalition of Freedom of Religion and Belief which was founded in 1998 as an international extension of Norway's Council for Religious and Life Stance Communities. In the Coalition, Norwegian Christians, Muslims, Jews, Buddhists and secular humanists have collaborated with like-minded partners in other parts of the world – in a common commitment to freedom of religion, protection of minorities and interreligious dialogue. In 2005 – ten years after the difficult case in 1995 – the Coalition sent a Muslim-Christian delegation to Pakistan. The aim of the visit was to learn more about the situation of religious minorities, to hear their views on current legislative issues, and critically discuss the Pakistani blasphemy law with religious leaders. When confronting conservative Muslims on the issue of blasphemy, it made no difference whether it was a Christian or Muslim who expressed the delegation's concerns. Being part of the delegation, I strongly felt that the foundation for the journey was a joint commitment to certain human rights values which were also (since we were from the same country) felt to be common 'Norwegian' values.

It was similar processes that led to a Christian-Muslim statement from 2009 titled 'Stop the violence against Christians in Pakistan', in which one 'expresses support and solidarity with Christians in Pakistan who are harassed and fear for their life and health'. With an interesting coupling of secular and religious language, the signatories 'encourage Norwegians to express support and solidarity with the Christians in Pakistan who are exposed to violence, also through prayers in church services and in mosques'.[16]

What has evolved through these sometimes quite demanding dialogues is a common commitment not only to exposed minority groups but also (to some degree) in relation to vulnerable individuals. In 2007, the Christian-Muslim Contact Group issued a joint Christian-Muslim statement which also evoked international attention; namely about the right to change one's religion. In this statement, Christians and Muslims jointly promise to protect those who embark upon the risk project of changing one's religion:

> The Islamic Council of Norway and the Church of Norway Council on Ecumenical and International Relations jointly declare that everyone is free to adopt the religious faith of their choice. We denounce, and are committed to counteracting all violence, discrimination and harassment inflicted in reaction to a person's conversion, or desire to convert, from one religion to another, be it in Norway or abroad.[17]

Although the basic message is moulded in human rights language, the joint statement also refers to the respective religious resources, although without any further elaboration on the legal and theological reasoning underlying their conclusion:

> We interpret our religious traditions such that everyone has the right to freely choose their religious belief and faith community, and to practice their religion publicly as well as privately.

Mutual understanding – even empathy – seems actually to be just as weighty an argument as the non-explicated religious reference above:

> As religious communities we experience joy within our respective contexts whenever a person wishes to share our faith and join our religious community. Therefore we also respect a person's right to convert to a different religion than our own.

In my understanding, the joint statement on the right to conversion illustrates interreligious dialogue's 'secular' orientation towards a common, ethical language – with shared humanity as the common horizon. To the extent that religious resources are referred to, it serves to underpin the common argument.

If the above can be taken as representative, it seems fair to conclude that Christian-Muslim dialogue has taken quite a few steps away from religious group interests, in the direction of a human rights commitment that challenges traditional attitudes within the religions.

Another recurrent theme in the Contact Group's work has been the situation of women in religious cultures, linking up with long-term work for the empowerment of women in Western churches and the emerging 'gender jihad'[18] in Muslim cultures. In the same year as the Contact Group published a book titled 'Dialogue with and without veil' (Grung and Larsen 2000) a painful conversation (also for the Contact Group) about female genital mutilation erupted in the wake of a television documentary in 2000 which (by use of a hidden camera) revealed support for female circumcision among some African imams. The then leader of the Islamic Council (one of those who were interviewed) was understood not to oppose female circumcision strongly enough, and resigned. In response to his resignation, the Islamic Council decided to elect the female Norwegian convert Lena Larsen as their new president (probably the first-ever female president of a representative Islamic body).

Then, in 2009, the Christian-Muslim Contact Group issued a joint declaration against violence in close relationships.[19] In this joint statement, violence against women is characterized as 'brutal breaches of fundamental human rights' and 'criminal deeds that violate both our religious teachings and human rights'. The entire statement is characterized by a double reference to religious teachings and human rights. Although religious resources for combating domestic violence were not explicated in the statement itself, one Christian and one Muslim theological reflection on the problem of violence was attached to the statement.

Although religious resources are drawn upon, I would still argue that the statements' dominant orientation is towards human rights language – and a common ethical language which by virtue of its focus on vulnerable individuals can actually be characterized as humanistic. (In Chapter 8, I will pursue my reflections on the humanization of theology and ethics.)

If the dominant orientation is humanistic, interreligious dialogue certainly seems to stimulate *change* in the religions. One should probably not overestimate the potential for *general* change in what happens in a conversation between religious leaders, or between dialogue activists. It should, however, be noted that what the Christian-Muslim Contact Group expresses in public is the official view of the Church of Norway and of the Islamic Council. On the Muslim side, the cited statements about vulnerable minorities, the right to change one's faith, and violence in close relationships, have been thoroughly discussed in the (male-dominated) imam committee.

Yet there is no doubt that other, less human rights-friendly tendencies are well represented on both the Christian and the Muslim side (cf. Chapter 4). For instance, an investigation in 2011 into the political attitudes of Norwegian Muslim leaders revealed that some of the imams that had endorsed the 2007 joint statement on the right to convert did not fully agree on it as a global principle that was also applicable to Muslim societies (Elgvin 2011: 42f.). In any case, there is a long journey from the reciprocal changes that may occur in committed dialogue partners to more comprehensive processes of change in the religions. My point here is not to speculate about the range of influence of various forums for interfaith dialogue but, rather, to indicate a particular kind of *dynamics*; namely that interreligious dialogue in modern societies seems to draw strongly in the direction of a common language for life in the *saeculum*.

Secularity and the hermeneutics of love

I started this chapter with a reference to *A Common Word*'s summoning of Muslims and Christians to unite in the double commandment of love, as an example of how interreligious dialogue can be moulded in a distinctively religious language. The theme of love can also, however, be seen as offering a perspective on interreligious relations that emphasize the *emphatic* dimension of dialogue. In some of the recent literature about interreligious dialogue, established forms of interfaith conversation are criticized for being too rational in their approach. For instance, in a critical discussion of Hans Küng and the

Parliament of the World's Religions 'Declaration toward a global ethic' from 1993 (which will be further discussed in Chapter 4), David Cheetham notes that several theologians would ask: 'Can a secular ethic provoke love, mercy or even concern?' (2013: 166). Partly defending Hans Küng's and John Rawls' secular visions of a global ethic built on overlapping consensus between the religions, Cheetham nevertheless suggests that interreligious ethics should aim not so much at reaching 'a definite code of ethics with many signatories' but, rather, 'a space of creative responsibility between people':

> What if the vision of cooperation could be accomplished not so much by a declaration but by addressing the issue of interpersonal ethics and how it might take place in a diverse world? (Cheetham 2013: 170f, 156f.)

This is where Werner Jeanrond's notion of 'a hermeneutics of love' might come in. As Jeanrond notes, love is much more than empathy. While empathy refers to attitudes, love in the comprehensive sense 'involves affective, cognitive, critical, and self-critical dimensions of relationality' (Jeanrond 2010: 52). Applied on interreligious relations, a hermeneutics of love integrates respect for the other and for the self as other (in Ricoueur's sense). Seeing love as a deeply human capacity which far transcends the outlook of this or that religious tradition, Jeanrond suggests that '[a]ny encounter among human beings . . . entails the possibility for a loving encounter' (2010: 57).

The practical consequences of Cheetham's and Jeanrond's calls for 'creative responsibility' and an 'interreligious hermeneutics of love' are not crystal clear. They formulate a necessary caution, however, against any conception of the secular which – for instance, by over-focusing the rational element in dialogue – ends up as a reductionist discourse. The alternative, as emphasized by both of them, is not to become more 'religious' in dialogue, but rather more fully *human*.

4

The Image of the Other and Othering Discourses

From a historical or social science perspective, the emergence of interreligious dialogue in late modernity can hardly be understood unless in contrast with the simultaneous growth in confrontational identity politics in the name of religion. In academic contexts, the term 'identity politics' (Heyer 2012) designates strategies of political mobilization focused on one particular aspect of people's identity – be it gender, ethnicity, cultural or religious belonging. In his book *In the Name of Identity: Violence and the Need to Belong*, the French-Lebanese author Amin Maalouf (2000) explores the murderous potential of religious identity politics. Even in less violent forms, identity politics tends to blur the complexity of people's identity which, in real life, consists of a wide range of elements, each of which may be felt to be more or less important in shifting contexts and political circumstances.

Dialogue versus identity politics

With a view to Christian-Muslim relations, in most parts of the world dialogue activists vie for hegemony with proponents of religious identity politics and with media discourses that regularly draw in the direction of confrontation rather than conversation.

Among Christians in Norway, dialogical attitudes as expressed by the leaders of the established churches compete with anti-Islamic sentiments among ordinary church members and in Christian groups associated with the

New Christian Right. On the Muslim side, the dialogical stance of the broadly representative Islamic Council has been challenged by the more radical voices of young Muslims who have increasingly accused the Islamic Council of being too compromise-oriented in their dealings with other faith communities and the state authorities. For instance, during the controversy over the Danish cartoons in 2006, and in a similar conflict in 2010 when a newspaper reprinted an old cartoon depicting the Prophet as a pig, large demonstrations with confrontational rally cries were staged by Muslim activists who defied the explicit advice of the Islamic Council and their imam committee to seek the understanding of co-citizens instead of taking to the streets. The demonstrators, on the other hand, expressed strong feelings of alienation, proclaimed Islam as the only truth, and accused Norway of crusading against Muslims.[1] In 2012, in connection with protests against the film *Innocence of Muslims*, intra-Muslim conflict was further exposed when a new and radical group called 'The Prophet's Ummah' rallied some 100 people invoking the example of Osama bin Laden in a demonstration outside the American embassy, whereas simultaneously the Islamic Council gathered 6,000 people in a peaceful meeting which also included the Bishop of Oslo and the Mayor of Oslo.[2]

'The Other' and othering discourses

Constructions of the other may be seen as fundamental and hardly avoidable when establishing cultural and religious categories (Smith 2004: 230ff.). In this chapter, constructions of the other are dealt with in connection with markedly *confrontational* discourses. Trying to conceptualize confrontational tendencies in the religious communities, religious identity politics seems always to be nourished by othering discourses which depict the cultural or religious Other as a threat or enemy. Although speaking of the Other with a capital O has almost become an academic mania, the meaning is not always clear. In Levinas (cf. Chapter 2), relating to the Other is associated with respected difference and irreducible responsibility, even before God.[3] In the tradition of Edward Said and Simone de Beauvoir, the term connotes, rather, 'othering' in the sense of alienation and dissociation. Whereas Simone de Beauvoir's book about *The Second Sex* (from 1949) has informed later discourses on the gendered other,

Edward Said's critique in his book *Orientalism* (from 1978) relates to Western conceptions of the cultural (i.e. Eastern) other. With regard to conceptions of the cultural other, Orientalism can of course be inverted to Occidentalism, with no less stereotypical images of the West and Western people on the part of 'Easterners' (Buruma and Margalit 2004).

In trying to understand othering discourses, it is important to grasp how conceptions of (1) the Cultural Other, (2) the Gendered Other and (3) the Religious Other are intertwined and how they feed on each other.

As regards the religious Other, the competition between dialogical and confrontational discourses corresponds to some extent with the difference between *responding to* the Other in the spirit of Levinas, and *distancing oneself* from or subordinating the Other to Oneself in Said and de Beauvoir's sense.

Pre-modern and late modern othering of Islam and Judaism

Although Said and de Beauvoir's critiques of othering devices relate in the main to modern discourses, the aforementioned modes of othering have, of course, pre-modern antecedents. When trying to understand the grammar of contemporary anti-Islamic rhetoric in Christian circles, medieval tropes seem often to be replayed, although with some distinctively modern additions.

William Montgomery Watt has summarized the standard content of medieval Christian othering of Muslims in four points: (1) Islam is a religion that spreads by violence and the sword; (2) Islam is a religion of self-indulgence; (3) Islam is false and a deliberate perversion of truth; and (4) Muhammad is the Anti-Christ (Watt 1991: 85f.; with particular reference to Thomas Aquinas' and his contemporary theologians' perception of Islam).

This particular repertoire of accusations must of course be read in its medieval context of military clashes with Muslims in the crusades and the Spanish Reconquista, coupled with spiritual clashes between monastic Christianity and a more 'worldly' Islam. In these European developments, Islam might seem to be depicted as the dark shadow of Europe itself.

As for othering discourses about Islam in the contemporary context, two distinctive elements seem to be added to the medieval stereotypes: (1) a critique of Sharia, informed by modern human rights discourses, and (2) a critique of

Islam as a religion oppressive of women, informed by modern feminism and replacing the gendered elements in medieval critique of Islam as a religion of self-indulgence.

In Christian/European history, anti-Judaic stereotypes have been even cruder than the anti-Islamic ones, with a mainstream legacy of hate speech against the Jews which was only broken in the latter half of the twentieth century (Berg Eriksen, Harket and Lorenz 2005). Anti-Jewish sentiments still persist among relatively large groups of Europeans. A survey conducted by Pew Research Center in 2008 showed that 46 per cent of the Spanish, 36 per cent of the Polish, 34 per cent of the Russian, 25 per cent of the German but only 9 per cent of the British respondents expressed negative views about Jews. Questions about views of Muslims rendered quite similar tendencies and, in general, the survey indicated that negative views of Jews and Muslims seemed to be simultaneously on the rise in Europe.[4]

Just as anti-Judaism in the modern context has been merged with racism and expressed itself as secular anti-Semitism, anti-Islamic rhetoric as expressed by European Christians has been combined with ideas about the moral and political superiority of the modern West over against the perceived backwardness of Muslim cultures. Content-wise, several parallel features (such as conspiracy theories and accusations of disloyalty) can in fact be identified between present-day Islamophobia and European anti-Semitism (Bunzl 2007; Døving 2010).

Muslim othering of Jews and Christians

On the Muslim side, traditional anti-Jewish sentiments have been influenced by modern anti-Semitism which, from the 1930s, was promulgated by Europeans in the Arab world (Krämer 2006). In the twentieth century, anti-Jewish sentiments have also been spurred by Zionism and the establishment and further expansion of Israel. Thus, in present-day Muslim cultures, anti-Zionism may often be expressed in the form of anti-Judaism.

Although there is no continuous tradition of anti-Judaism in Muslim cultures, the fact that the Qur'an and other classical sources portray Jews (more than Christians) as adversaries of Muslims means that anti-Jewish sentiments may still be evoked with references to the foundational narratives of Islam (Leirvik 2011a). On the other hand, the classical sources also express recognition of Jews as (together with Christians) 'people of the book' and Muslim empires have a long tradition of state tolerance of Jewish communities. In some historical epochs, notably in mediaeval Spain, Muslims and Jews have also shared a sense of solidarity over against Christian princes and their violent Reconquista of Spain which resulted in forced conversions and eventually expulsion of both groups from the Iberian Peninsula.

As for Muslim polemics against Christians, classical accusations such as (Jews' and) Christians' alleged tampering with the scriptures (*tahrif*) were boosted by modern historical-critical approaches to the Bible in the West, allowing apologetically minded Muslims to attack Western missionaries 'with the weapons of their adversaries' (Schirrmacher 1992). The controversy over the so-called Gospel of Barnabas makes Muslim-Christian conversation about the Bible even more difficult, since so many Muslims treat what Western scholars regard as a sixteenth-century forgery (possibly of Morisco origin) as an authentic, early Christian Gospel (Leirvik 2010a: 132–44).

In another modern re-actualization of history, the Crusades (which contemporary Arab historians saw not as a religious war but as a Frankish onslaught) were transformed to a prime example of the perennial conflict between 'Christianity' and 'Islam'.

Fed by historical experiences as well as current conflicts, negative images of Jews and Christians seem to overrule memories of good neighbourliness in Muslim majority societies. A survey by the Pew Research Center from 2005 showed that negative views of Jews and Christians are widespread in Muslim majority societies. In Lebanon, which has a large Christian minority, 91 per cent of the public thought favourably of Christians. Smaller majorities in Jordan and Indonesia also had positive views of Christians. However, in Turkey (63%), Morocco (61%) and Pakistan (58%), a majority expressed negative opinions of Christians.

With regard to anti-Jewish attitudes, the situation seems to be even worse. According to the mentioned survey, anti-Jewish sentiment seemed almost to be endemic in the Muslim world. In Lebanon, all the Muslim respondents and 99 per cent of the Christians stated that they had a very unfavourable view of Jews. Similarly, 99 per cent of Jordanians had a unfavourable view of Jews, as did the majorities of Moroccans (88%), Indonesians (76%), Pakistanis (74%) and six out of ten Turks.[5]

But this is not the entire picture, at least not as regards Muslim perception of Christians. Other surveys indicate that Muslims living in Europe and the United States have more positive perceptions both of the West and of Christians. A survey by Pew from 2006 indicated quite clearly that French, German and Spanish Muslims were considerably less inclined to see Westerners as selfish, arrogant, violent, immoral, etc. than their fellow Muslims in Indonesia, Nigeria, Turkey and the Arab world.[6] It should be noted that non-Muslims interviewed in the same survey were, in general, just as inclined to attribute such negative characteristics to Muslims, with a slightly better image of Muslims in the United States and in Great Britain.[7]

Openness and othering as simultaneous tendencies

Just as interfaith dialogue and confrontational identity politics are simultaneous and competing phenomena on the global scene, dialogical openness and othering discourses might seem to coexist even in individual faith communities (both on the Muslim and the Christian side).

One example is the Pakistani-based organization Minhaj ul-Qur'an. In the 1980s, its leader Tahir ul-Qadri visited Scandinavia several times, with ensuing reports published by his organization of how he completely silenced his Christian interlocutors in rather polemical dialogues staged by his organization. His polemics from this period resemble that of Ahmed Deedat (Westerlund 2003). In his pamphlet *Islam and Christianity* from 1986, Tahir ul-Qadri conventionally pinpoints the 'contradictions in the Bible', and also rallies the Gospel of Barnabas in his attacks on the authenticity of the New Testament (Leirvik 2010a: 156).

Some 15 years later, Tahir ul-Qadri appears hand in hand with the Norwegian-based global evangelist Aril Edvardsen (d. 2008) and local charismatic Christians in Pakistan, reading from the Sermon on the Mount in a huge evangelical meeting staged by Edvardsen (Leirvik 2006d). After publishing a 600-pages fatwa against terrorism in 2010, Tahir ul-Qadri engaged leaders from other religions to sign the so-called London Declaration for Global Peace and Resistance against Extremism in which one can read:

> Jews, Muslims, Christians, Hindus, Buddhists and those of other religions, along of course with all people who do not identify with any faith, must enjoy the same civil and legal rights and freedoms and be able to live in peace and harmony and must pursue peace only through mutually respectful engagement and dialogue.[8]

Likewise, in the Norwegian context, representatives of Minhaj ul-Qur'an have been at the forefront of Muslim-Christian dialogue and cooperation. But Tahir ul-Qadri's polemical pamphlet against Christianity is still on display and for sale in their mosque in Oslo.

How should this be interpreted? Are we witnessing a steady development from confrontation to dialogue, or a simultaneous presence of opposite tendencies? The same question arose from a study of the mosque literature and web pages of the Islamic Cultural Centre, a mosque in Oslo with roots in the Pakistani Jamaat-e-Islami movement (Christensen 2010). Among the literature that is still spread by the mosque (and to some extent, posted on their web pages), in 2010 one could still find translations of books by the organization's founder Maulana Abu Ala Maududi and the ideologue Hammudah Abdulati, articulating a mixed cultural, gendered and religious othering of the West and of Christianity. In their books, the cultural and religious Other (Westerners, Christians) are often portrayed as unbelievers (*kuffar*) and as immoral people with whom one should not socialize. Abdulati's book *Introduction to Islam* promotes polygamy and depicts the status of modern women in the West as an example of the cultural Other's moral decay. After the Norwegian version of the book was criticized publicly, the electronic version was eventually removed from the organization's web pages.

Also, in other pamphlets available at the Islamic Cultural Centre in the last couple of decades, the approach to other religions has been markedly apologetic and the mosque has occasionally invited such speakers as Abdul Raheem Green and the converted pastor Yusuf Estes.

On the other hand, the Islamic Cultural Centre has long been a stronghold for dialogue activists. Their mosque in Oslo is called 'Centre for dialogue and knowledge' and their dialogical profile can also be spotted at their web pages.

A cultural festival hosted by the mosque in 2009 explicitly invited Christian groups to present themselves, in conjunction with a self-critical recognition that 'it's time that Muslims learn more about Christians'.

The study referred to above (Christensen 2010) also revealed critical attitudes among some young adult leaders towards the older generations' use of Abdulati's and Maududi's books. When in 2010 the mosque published the first volume of its new Norwegian translation of the Qur'an – based on Maududi's translation and commentary in Urdu and English – they boldly edited Maududi's view on punishment, stating in a footnote that the qur'anic verse 4: 34 can never be used as a legitimation of any kind of violence against women. But, at the same time, Maududi's other books continued to be spread unaltered by the mosque.

Again we can see how seemingly contradictory tendencies coexist in the same mosque, in a complex renegotiation of past profiles in which living dialogue with people of other faiths and conviction in the West seems to be the motor of change. Alongside Muslim stereotypes about (Western) Christians, and corresponding Western and Christians' perceptions of Muslims, it should of course be noted that intra-Muslim and intra-Christian stereotypes may be just as ingrained as the interreligious ones. For instance, research at the Faculty of Theology in Oslo has revealed how relatively secularized young Bosnian Muslims in Oslo see Pakistanis as the stereotypical Other (Bruun 2008) and how young Shi'ite Muslims see Sunni Muslims in general as more liable to extremism (Strandhagen 2008). Correspondingly, a study of Christian and Muslim leaders' perception of each other in Ghana demonstrated that intra-Muslim and intra-Christian suspicion seemed to be just as much to the forefront as the mutual stereotypes between Muslims and Christians (Asinor 2006).

Christian othering of Muslims

As for anti-Islamic sentiments in Europe as well as in the United States, recent developments indicate that secular forces and the New Christian right have forged rhetorical as well as political alliances against the perceived Islamic threat. The report *Fear, Inc. The Roots of the Islamophobia Network in America*

(Ali et al. 2011) gives ample evidence of such alliances on the United States' part when documenting which persons, organizations and institutions have taken the lead in the last decade's 'creeping Sharia' discourse.

Secular-Christian alliances against Islam

In my interpretation, similar alliances were struck in the Scandinavian context during the Danish cartoon controversy in 2005–6 (Leirvik 2011c). The cartoons that were considered most offensive depicted Muhammad as a violent figure, oppressive of women – fully in line with standard anti-Islamic rhetoric in the modern context. In his book 'Threatened by Islamists' (2006) Vebjørn Selbekk (the editor of *Magazinet* which republished the Danish cartoons in Norway) reproduced stereotypes about Islam as a violent, undemocratic religion which is also repressive of women. Although Selbekk declared his inspiration from the New Christian Right in the United States,[9] in his critique of Islam he leaned more on secular critics such as the self-proclaimed apostates Ibn Warraq and Ayaan Hirsi Ali (2006: 215).

Content-wise, the critique of Islam by former Muslims and by secular neoconservatives (cf. *Fear, Inc.*) is more or less identical with that of representatives of the New Christian Right – only with a stronger focus among secularized critics on the oppression of women.

Another element in merging New Christian Right and neoconservative discourses is the combination of anti-Islamic and pro-Israel stances – strikingly revealed in John Hagee's book *Jerusalem Countdown* (2006), a book that combines apocalyptic visions of Israel being threatened by its enemies with the 'unveiling' of Islam as an inherently violent religion. The main source of Hagee's attack on Islam appears to be the books of the convert from Islam Mark A. Gabriel, in particular *Islam and Terrorism. What the Qur'an Really Teaches about Christianity, Violence and the Goals of the Islamic Jihad* (2002) and *Islam and the Jews. The Unfinished Battle* (2003). Like Hagee's book, Gabriel's works have been published by Front Line and Charisma House, both of which are publishing houses under the Strang Communications Company in Florida.[10] Behind these publishers one will find the international movement Youth With A Mission (YWAM), to which Mark A. Gabriel has been attached since his conversion from Islam to Christianity. Correspondingly, in Norway, Gabriel's books have been published by Prokla Media, the publishing house of YWAM's national branch Ungdom i Oppdrag which has thus been an important contributor to the anti-Islamic rhetoric of NCR groups in Norway.

In *Islam and Terrorism,* Gabriel puts forward the conventional argument in NCR circles about Islam as an inherently violent religion. He insists that militant Muslims' interpretation of the Qur'an is the most authentic one, characterizes Islamic history as 'a river of blood' and warns Christians against dialogue-seeking Muslims who must be suspected of hiding their real agenda, which is taking control of the West.

In the perspective of Youth With A Mission, their spiritual-war approach to Islam has been linked with fervent support of Israel, sometimes in an apocalyptic perspective, as one can also see in Hagee's aforementioned book. In a 2003 newsletter of YWAM Norway, in connection with the launch of the Norwegian edition of Gabriel's book *Islam and the Jews*, their leader Alv Magnus offered the following perspective: 'Islam is a spiritual power. It keeps millions as captives in spiritual darkness, denies Christ and opposes God's plans for Israel and the Jews.'[11]

The New Christian Right in alliance with the right-wing populism

The Norwegian translation of Gabriel's Islam and terrorism has been one of the bestselling books about Islam in the first decade of the 2000s. When published in 2003, it was also distributed free to all members of the Norwegian parliament. Here, it was eagerly picked up by Carl I. Hagen, the then chairman of the Progress Party, which in polls and in their most successful elections have attracted some 20 per cent of Norwegian voters.

Indicative of an emerging alliance between NCR and the Progress Party, its chairman Carl I. Hagen in a televised debate in November 2004 pointed to Gabriel's book as one of most reliable sources on Islam.[12] Some months before, Hagen made big headlines after his visit to the charismatic 'Living Word' congregation in Bergen, which was already known for the connections between some of their members and the Progress Party in Bergen. In his Living Word address in the summer of 2004, Hagen was applauded by his Christian audience when praising Israel and characterizing Muhammad as a warlord.[13] In his autobiography from 2007, he repeats his characterization of

Muhammad as 'the warlord, assailant and abuser of women . . . who murdered and accepted rape as a means of conquest' (Hagen 2007: 539).[14]

Hagen's speech in Living Word was probably the first example of him using the expression 'we Christians' as a mature expression of his growing insistence that 'Christian values and culture are challenged by Islam', as expressed in a Parliamentary document from 1999–2000 (Brekke 2004: 121).

Personalized othering of Islam and Muslims

In tune with modernity's focus on personalities, the image of the Muslim Other as depicted by confrontational Christian seems increasingly to be focused on the person of Muhammad. One of Mark Gabriel's books, *Jesus and Muhammad. Profound Differences and Surprising Similarities* (2004), illustrates amply the tendency to contrast Muhammad with Jesus (as in chairman Hagen's 2004 speech, referred to above). Searching the internet for 'Jesus and Muhammad', one will find a number of Christian apologetic websites with rather crude comparisons of the two figures, not surprisingly to the great benefit of Jesus. In a website posted by an organization called Christian Apologetics and Research Ministry, we find for instance the following comparisons:

> Jesus never killed anyone; Muhammad killed many.
>
> Jesus owned no slaves; Muhammad owned slaves.
>
> Jesus spoke well of women; Muhammad said women were 1/2 as smart as men and that the majority in hell will be women.
>
> Jesus never married; Muhammad had over 20 wives and even married a nine year old girl.
>
> Jesus performed many miracles; Muhammad's only alleged miracle was the Quran.
>
> Jesus was virgin born; Muhammad was not virgin born.
>
> Jesus died and rose from the dead; Muhammad died and stayed dead.[15]

Apart from the rather banal 'theological' comparisons, polemical comparisons of this kind indicate how undeniable differences in the two prophets' career, as reflected in the classical sources, are transformed into antagonistic contradictions which block any meaningful conversation about themes such as religion and politics, myth and historical truth, and the relation between historical images and contemporary identity discourses.

In polemical comparisons, portraits of Jesus and Muhammad bleed into implied images of the stereotypical Muslim and of the idealized Christian respectively. Images of the foundational figures of Christianity and Islam can therefore not be isolated from contemporary identity discourses.

Othering discourses are obviously a joint challenge for Christians and Muslims in particular. Dialogical responses to mutual polemics need to take into account the whole spectrum of cultural, gendered and religious perceptions that feed into the rhetoric of confrontational ideologues and underlie dominant media discourses. One needs to face the Other in his or her complexity, and to be honest about one's own inner wavering between recognition and suspicion.

In interfaith dialogue, religious differences must not be isolated from other relevant differences such as gender, class and culture. Only by addressing differences in their complexity can one avoid the compartmentalization fallacy of identity politics, taking instead complex differences and complex attitudes as a challenge (Grung 2011b).

Stereotypes coming true?

Although Christians and Muslims committed to dialogue will often feel the need to defend each other publicly against unjust characterizations, interfaith dialogue must also face the uncomfortable fact of stereotypes coming true. Both Christian and Muslim do, in fact (as implied in conspiracy theories) often struggle to 'Christianize' or 'Islamicize' their environments, either by defending historical majority positions (as reflected in many constitutions) or demanding legal changes to their benefit when in the minority. Christian right-wing politicians and conservative evangelists (not to mention extremists such as the Norwegian perpetrator of a massacre on 22 July 2011, who draws heavily on Templar imagery in his manifesto) use crusader rhetoric when promoting their cause.

On the Muslim side, widespread attitudes in the Muslim world do seem to confirm the apprehensions of neoconservative ideologues warning against 'creeping Sharia'. For instance, a Pew survey from 2010 showed that four out of five Egyptians and Pakistanis supported harsh punishment such as amputations and stoning/death penalty for theft, adultery and apostasy, against approximately one-third of Indonesians and 10–15 per cent of Turks.[16] Similar numbers could be found in a Pew survey on 'The World's Muslims: Religion, Politics and Society' from 2013, only with a higher percentage of Indonesians supporting physical punishments.[17] Although such figures can seldom be taken at face value, Christians and Muslims committed to dialogue in a Western context can hardly overlook the global realities behind these responses.

Only by being honest about the unpleasant can dialogue take a firm step forward and hope to influence the general public. That is why joint statements by Christians and Muslims in the European context on highly controversial issues such as the right to change one's religion (cf. Chapter 3), or Tariq Ramadan's 2005 moratorium on physical punishments[18] (cf. Chapter 8) are so important, although accusations of lip-service to Western values are often levelled against those Muslims in the West who take a markedly different stand on what are thought to be standard Muslim views globally.

In such cases, dialogue-minded Christians often feel called to defend their Muslim partners publicly, against populist perceptions of Islam and deliberate vilification of Muslims by anti-Islamic ideologues.

5

Faith-based Diplomacy and Interfaith Activism: Dialogue from Above and Below

From the beginning of the 1990s, the world has witnessed a simultaneous growth in religious identity politics (in part, violent) and interfaith dialogue (partly centred on the concept of a global ethic). In the following, I will exemplify the dual tendencies with reference to two documents of a rather different inclination from 1993 before I go on to discuss different kinds of dialogical responses to confrontational identity politics – be it dialogue from above or from below.

Conflict between civilizations, or global ethic?

In 1993, two influential documents on religion, conflict and global ethics were published, both of them receiving a great deal of international attention. The first was the American political scientist Samuel Huntington's article in *Foreign Affairs* on 'The Clash of Civilizations?' (1993) which was later expanded to a book (1996). Under the impression of an emerging political Islam, the First Gulf War and the Balkan wars, Huntington prophesied that future conflicts will follow the cultural fault lines between the seven or eight 'civilizations' he enumerated, particularly those between the 'Islamic' and 'Western' civilizations. His most infamous formulation in that respect was the generalized contention that 'Islam has bloody borders' (Huntington 1993: 35).

Huntington also confirmed old ideas about the West's civilizing mission and encouraged Western agents to conduct a global value politics based on ideals such as individualism, human rights, the separation between state and religion, free markets and liberal democracy. In his seminal essay, Huntington emphasized that such value-based politics should not be understood as an idealistic project – defending and promoting these values are actually in the West's best interest. Huntington thus combined value-based and interest-based (realpolitik-oriented) politics, inspiring among other American neoconservative thinkers and their vision of 'liberalism with teeth'. Implying the rest of world is considerably more 'religious' than the West, he also foresaw that the West's renewed civilizational mission would be met with religion-based resistance:

> [T]he efforts of the West to promote its values of democracy and liberalism to universal values, to maintain its military predominance and to advance its economic interests engender countering responses from other civilizations. Decreasingly able to mobilize support and form coalitions on the basis of ideology, governments and groups will increasingly attempt to mobilize support by appealing to common religion and civilization identity. (Huntington 1993: 29)

From these formulations, it is hard to avoid the impression of an othering of non-Westerners as more fervently religious than the people and politicians in the West. Despite his othering discourses and conflict-oriented scenarios, however, it should be noted that Huntington also realized the need 'to identify elements of commonality between Western and other civilizations'. For the relevant future, he suggests, there will be no universal civilization, 'but instead a world of different civilizations, each of which will have to learn to coexist with the others' (Huntington 1993: 49).

It is still not clear from Huntington's reasoning what it would mean for international relations to develop a form of coexistence based on 'elements on commonality' as well as respected differences. Another influential document on religion, politics and ethics published in 1993 was the so-called Declaration towards a Global Ethic drafted by the German Catholic theologian Hans Küng (founder of 'The Global Ethic Foundation') for the Parliament of the World's Religions' gathering in Chicago (Küng 1995: 7–26). The Declaration, which was signed by a large group of religious leaders and dialogue activists, is unambiguously focused on commonalities rather than differences. Distinguishing between 'ethic' (a basic moral attitude) and 'ethics' (philosophical or theological theories of moral attitudes, values and norms), Hans Küng suggests that a global ethic must be neither too vague nor too detailed. In a completely different tone from that of Huntington's conflict-oriented article, the Declaration unfolds a vision of a global society founded on the Golden Rule's universal principle of reciprocity (all you would have others do to you, you also do to them). The document also indicates that the time-honoured, ethical principles of the world's religions can be reinterpreted so as to become the foundation for a global culture. In conjunction with central commandments in the Jewish-Christian tradition as well as in Buddhist ethics, the Declaration speaks of 'four irrevocable directives': (1) You shall not kill: Commitment to a culture of non-violence and respect for life; (2) You shall not steal: Commitment to a culture of solidarity and a just economic order; (3) You shall not lie: Commitment to a culture of tolerance and a life of truthfulness; (4) You shall not commit sexual immorality: Commitment to a culture of equal rights and partnership between men and women.

In this Declaration, there are not many traces of realpolitik but no scarcity of lofty ideals. It should be noted, however, that in his other works Hans Küng demonstrates how he relates his concept of a global ethic to a 'a new paradigm in international relations' (2008). Differently from the realpolitik-oriented dictated peace after World War I, the world after 1945 witnesses the development of visions of global solidarity symbolized by the United Nations, the Universal Declaration of Human Rights (with subsequent human rights conventions) and the European Union, *competing with* the terror balance between East and West. After 1989, Küng sees a similar competition between disarmament and regional cooperation (in the direction of further European integration), *competing with* a US-dominated 'new world order' and Huntington's perceived 'clash of civilizations'. For Küng, this is the overall pattern in which it makes sense to speak of a global ethic that is more morally binding than the legally oriented human rights conventions, although based on the same values.

Deductive and inductive approaches

The Declaration towards a global ethic represents a *deductive* approach to interreligious dialogue, in that it builds on certain values that may be deduced from the ethical teachings of the world's religions. In what he terms 'a sympathetic critique' of the Declaration, Paul Hedges raises the question of whether it is founded on principles or practices. It seems to draw, Hedges notes, on an essentialist picture of the world's religions rather than on 'a multitude of regional or local ethics with which we can work' (2008: 161).

A different, more *inductive* approach to the question of global ethics can be found in the Swedish theologian's Elisabeth Gerle's book *In Search of a Global Ethics* (1995), which was published two years after the global ethic declaration. With reference to ecumenical dialogues, she calls for a more contextual and process-oriented approach to global ethics. Venturing beyond general values and attitudes, Gerle speaks of 'ethics' and not of 'ethic'. She launches two clearly interrelated critiques of the deductive, 'universal values' approach. First, she notes that '[t]he asymmetry of the world complicates the notion of the universal ... The asymmetry has to do with power and participation giving some groups more choices and more influence than others' (Gerle 1995: 19).

Secondly, and in conjunction with feminist insights, she suggests that *relatedness* rather than abstract values should be the point of departure for the search for a global ethics. With Seyla Benhabib, she calls for a contextually sensitive universalism which is *interactive* rather than conceptual (Benhabib 1992: 3; Gerle 1995: 38f.), putting the stress on groups of people acting together faced with joint challenges.

Gerle seems to be advocating an inductive moral approach to pressing challenges that are unprecedented in nature and global in range. To survive in dignity and justice, people everywhere must engage in formulating a global ethics which surpasses traditional confines and the commonalities of 'basic attitudes'.

Many of the examples of interreligious dialogue given in this book take an inductive and interactive approach to dialogue, starting out from joint concerns in one's own context and trying to formulate concrete responses on an interreligious basis.

In the following discussion of religion and politics, the difference between deductive and inductive approaches should be kept in mind. The difference does not entirely coincide with that between dialogue from above or from below (cf. the subtitle of this chapter). Taken together, however, the distinction between deductive and inductive approaches and the difference between dialogue from above and below, may help to analyse who is laying the premises for concrete dialogue initiatives and whether dialogues can be said to be interactive or not.

From neglect of religion to faith-based diplomacy?

The two documents from 1993 – the one conflict-oriented, the other oriented towards dialogue – indicate how the discussion about international relations at the beginning of the 1990s was gradually focusing more than before on religion and values. In 1994, the year after Huntington's article and Küng's manifesto were published, the American political scientist and dialogue activist Douglas Johnston, with co-editor Cynthia Sampson, published a book titled *Religion, the Missing Dimension of Statecraft* (1994). Johnston argued that American foreign policy and diplomacy would have to take religion seriously to a greater extent as a political factor. He implies that the constitutional distinction between state and church in the United States may have made politicians blind to the political role of religious leaders and faith-based organizations: 'I concluded, rightly or wrongly, that the rigorous separation of church and state in the United States had so relegated religion to the realm of the personal that it left many of us insensitive to the extent to which religion and politics intertwine in much of the rest of the world' (1994: ix).

Ten years later, in 2003, Johnston published a new book, with a more (from his viewpoint) optimistic title: *Faith-based Diplomacy. Trumping Realpolitik*. The concluding chapter was written by history professor R. Scott Appleby, under the title 'Retrieving the missing dimension of statecraft: religious faith in the service of peace building'. Most of the book's chapters are case studies of religion's conflict enhancing or peace-building role in Kashmir, Sri Lanka, Israel and Palestine, the Balkans, and in Sudan. The book also discusses the peace-building potential of the world's religions from a more historical perspective. Samuel Huntington is referred to only in passing, but with affirmation when Johnston expresses his agreement that many of today's conflicts are of a cultural nature and that religion, 'as Samuel Huntington has pointed out . . . is the defining element of culture' (2003: 24). Critics will probably point out that the use of the definite article in the cited reference to Huntington – 'religion is the defining element of culture' – indicates that Johnston and his intellectual relatives put so much emphasis on religion's political role that other cultural and social factors are left entirely in the shade.

The central concept in Johnston's book is 'faith-based diplomacy', a phrase that has played a central role in internal US debates on whether governments can support 'faith-based' social work, without challenging the constitutionality separation between state and church. An example from the field of domestic policies is the White House Office on Faith-Based and Community Initiatives which was established by George W. Bush in 2001, and that Barack Obama took over but reorganized. While Bush in his implementation of faith-based policies focused strongly on so-called family values, Obama seemed rather to associate faith-based work with a commitment to social justice – thus illustrating that faith-based commitment may have quite different political expressions, both in domestic and foreign policies.

In the last decade, the term 'faith-based' has abounded in discussions about religion and politics, reflected also in the increased use of expressions such as 'faith-based organizations' (FBOs, as a particular form of NGOs). As regards the term 'faith-based diplomacy', Johnston and his co-authors place great emphasis on the personal qualifications and the deep religious knowledge that must be acquired in order – as a 'track one' diplomat or 'track two' dialogue worker – to play a constructive role in conflicts where different religions and often a whole arsenal of religious leaders with different agendas may be involved. In line with the vision underlying the US National Prayer Breakfast institution, where Johnston himself has been involved, Johnston emphasizes that a faith-based peace worker must be able to draw actively on the spiritual resources of the religions.

Faith-based problems

Several examples could be mentioned from the last decade of how governments have supported 'faith-based' attempts at conflict resolution and peace building in areas where religion is an apparent part of the conflict pattern. For instance, since the late 1990s the Norwegian government has supported individual, faith-based diplomats (mostly Norwegian church leaders) who have facilitated peace-building efforts and interreligious networking in places such as East Timor and the Holy Land. Support has also been given to such institutions as the European Council of Religious Leaders (a subsection of Religions for Peace), the Oslo Coalition on Freedom of Religion or Belief and the Islamic Council of Norway (in connection with their efforts at appeasement of angry Muslims in the Middle East and Pakistan after the cartoon clashes in 2005–6).

The establishment of regular forums for interreligious dialogue (such as the Council of Religious Institutions in the Holy Land[1]), in which confidence-building between religious leaders and attempts at conflict resolution may take place, is undoubtedly of great value. But as critics of the concept of faith-based diplomacy have pointed out, there are also some inherent problems in this way of acting. First, there is a risk that dialogue forums created on the initiative of governments or by using 'diplomatic' agents are not perceived as equally binding as dialogue initiatives taken by the religious leaders against the background of felt needs. Second, by engaging high-level religious leaders one also risks supporting leaders who often have markedly conservative attitudes in traditional value questions (e.g. when it comes to the place of women), to the detriment of other religious actors who have a more liberal, human rights-oriented and perhaps even a more socially radical agenda.

The question of which values a faith-based involvement actually supports is particularly pressing in the field of religion and development. Many examples can be cited – for instance, from African contexts – of how Christians, Muslims and practitioners of traditional religions may join hands in local community development, building on inclusive religious leadership as well as on the resources of traditional festivals (Etikpah 2010).

But there are also problems with basing community development on established structures of religious leadership. In an article from 2011 titled 'Religion and development. A practitioner's perspective on instrumentalization', Cassandra Balchin gives some examples of how aid organizations, in their well-meant attempt to engage religious leaders, may end up supporting a neoliberal privatization agenda that renders faith-based organizations with welfare responsibilities instead of governments, and enhances the power of established religious organizations that are often expressly critical of the idea of universal, non-discriminatory rights for vulnerable groups like women, gays and religious minorities.

Another problem with the concept of faith-based development or peace-building is the risk of marginalizing more secular parties. As Balchin puts it: 'By privileging religion, development policy of this type ignores rights struggles that are not framed with reference to religion – including rights demands that are based on concepts of citizenship' (2011: 17).

In both peace-building efforts and development work, responsible actors must realize that religious leaders hold very different views in moral and political questions. Some hold that women and religious minorities have only limited rights, in relation to men and the dominant religious tradition in the community. Other religious leaders think in terms of human rights principles and fight for universal, non-discriminatory rights. In the UN system, the two fronts stand against each other, and the dividing lines in contested value issues do not coincide with religious differences. For instance, conservative Christian lobby groups may seek alliances with Mormons and Muslim diplomats in order to protect 'family values' against feminist attacks and thus prevent what they see as radical interpretations of the UN's Convention against all forms of discrimination of women (Butler 2006). At the same time, we can also see the liberal groups ally with each other across the borders of faith, not least in the work for women's (in part also gay) rights.

Even in some global forums for religious dialogue that have been established in recent decades, one may observe how conservative tendencies (cue: 'gathering around traditional values') compete with more liberal attitudes (cue: 'commitment to universal human rights') in critical issues relating to gender justice, gay rights and the situation of religious minorities. An interesting example of how these two approaches may be (strenuously?) combined is a joint declaration on 'Advancing Human Dignity through Human Rights and Traditional Values' from 2011 by the European Council of Religious Leaders. Having noted that certain 'traditional values . . . which are widely held in religions and cultures . . . have been foundational in providing moral bases for societies' and that the Universal Declaration of Human Rights 'has contributed greatly to the furthering of human dignity in recent decades', the Council nevertheless observes a potential conflict between these two value traditions. The language of human rights may be misused 'to promote agendas that are inconsistent with human dignity', and 'specific expressions of human rights may conflict with specific traditional moral values' (ECRL 2011). Exactly which conflicts the religious leaders have in mind is not spelled out clearly but from similar discourses in other forums one might suspect that they have to do with gender and sexuality. Other interreligious declarations are more outspoken in a conservative direction. In July 2008, the Muslim World League – headed by Saudi Arabia's King Abdullah – hosted a 'World Conference on Dialogue' in Madrid at which King Juan Carlos I was also present. The participants represented a wide range of religious and cultural traditions. The Final Declaration was pre-composed and, although it has been available in different versions, the participants were not invited to discuss individual formulations. Three points indicated the markedly conservative character of this initiative, with the aim of protecting heavenly religions' symbols and their high status, the institution of the family from disintegration and society 'from deviant behaviors'.[2]

Dialogue from above and below

The cited examples of faith-based initiatives – aimed at development, peace-building or interreligious cooperation – are all taken from above, initiated either by governments or bodies of high-ranking religious leaders. Other faith-based initiatives have a different orientation – towards realities on the ground, or in critical distance to religious and political power structures.

Militants for peace

R. Scott Appleby, who contributed to Johnston's *Faith-based diplomacy*, has also developed an alternative notion that is less diplomatic. I'm referring to his concept of 'militants for peace' which he unfolded in *The Ambivalence of the Sacred* (1999; cf. Appleby 1998), with special reference to Buddhist monks and peace activists in South-East Asia.

Critically aware of the religions' historical ambivalence in relation to violence, Appleby focuses on non-violent activists in the history of religions who in different ways opposed the established powers. From a historical perspective, he notes that '[r]eligious radicals of the Christian Reformation condemned coercion in matters of religion and were prominent among the early modern proponents of religious liberty and freedom of speech'. In the twentieth century, he observes,

> Hindu and Christian religious leaders, including martyrs for peace such as Mohandas K. Gandhi and Martin Luther King Jr., were the most influential pioneers of nonviolence as both a spiritual practice and a political strategy. Islam, Judaism, and Buddhism have produced their own nonviolent militants and peacemakers. (Appleby 1999: 5)

The notion 'militants for peace' is of course chosen as an antonym to extremist militants who do not hesitate to use violence to obtain their goals. Instead of seeing non-violent activism as a 'moderate' form of religion, Appleby notes that '[b]oth types "go to extremes" of self-sacrifice in devotion to the sacred; both claims to be "radical", or rooted in and renewing the fundamental truths of their religious traditions' (1999: 44).

From a sociopolitical perspective, the activism of 'militants for peace' can also be seen as subversive of the established order – quite opposite to the usual connotations of 'diplomacy' (faith-based or not). Whereas diplomacy is conducted from above, non-violent militancy evolves from below. The same is true of different forms of interreligious dialogue. They may emerge from established religious and political power structures (from above), or take the form of potentially subversive activism (from below).

Critical civility

Another notion that captures the tension between dialogue from above and from below, is that of 'critical civility'. The notion has been developed by Iselin Frydenlund (2013). Based on empirical material from India, Sri Lanka and Rwanda, she seeks to understand the interaction between religious leaders and their socio-religious communities.

Whereas the notion of civility has close associations with customary etiquette and good manners, as also reflected in the expression 'civilized behaviour', Frydenlund seeks a qualified notion of civility reserved for understanding 'particular ways in which religious actors engage in community reconstruction in times of violent conflict, particularly at the local level' (2013: 109).

Behind her choice of the notion of 'critical civility' lies the recognition that civility may be more than etiquette: 'Civility can be regarded as a moral virtue because it implies consideration of others' feelings, engaging in tolerant restraint, gratitude and politeness.' What she calls critical civility, denotes 'a certain courteous behaviour in contexts in which such behaviour otherwise is not expected, or cannot be taken for granted'. More specifically, and with reference to empirical examples, she refers to 'ideas and practices in which members of one group transcend the boundaries of their community to show empathy or human suffering in defined out-groups' (2013: 120).

In this way, the notion of critical civility combines in an interesting way 'diplomatic' and 'subversive' approaches to religious conflict. Critical civility is potentially subversive in that it takes a critical view on social norms which tend to restrict solidarity to one's in-group, in situations of acute crisis and a sense of urgency.

Thus critical civility is also distinguished from mere political civility in that critical civility, by its readiness to disobeying established social and political norms, 'may or may not comply with liberal democratic values' (and, one might add, more diplomatic forms of intervention).

Multiculturalism and transreligious activism

The notions of 'militants for peace' and 'critical civility' both refer to the controversial nature of religious activism, as it unfolds within a particular tradition or transreligiously.

How should one see the relation between value-based and justice-oriented activism on the one hand, and multiculturalism on the other? In a book about 'the politics of separation', the Danish researchers Eriksen and Stjernfelt associate multiculturalism with identity politics, in that multiculturalist policies (in their view) tend to operate with rather closed notions of cultural and religious belonging (2009). This understanding of multiculturalism – as an attempt to secure the interests of neatly separated groups – differs considerably from more dynamic understandings of the politics of inclusion which seek to balance group rights with individual rights, in the analytical perspective of 'cultural complexity' (Hylland Eriksen 2009).

In situations of cultural complexity, multiple forms of belonging and competing interests across religious and cultural divides challenge more stable notions of diversity underlying multiculturalist policies. As noted by Anne Hege Grung (2011b), the discussion about multiculturalism and cultural complexity also poses a challenge for interreligious dialogue. Do various forms of dialogue simply cement established group patterns, only in a more friendly way than in confrontational identity politics, or does dialogue transcend the static notions of difference that are often seen as characteristic of multiculturalism?

With reference to interreligious dialogue, it is clear that many forms of institutionalized dialogue maintain a greater degree of group identity and group representation than cultural complexity-oriented modes of thinking about society. In many forms of dialogue, however, simplified forms of group identification (for instance, as 'Christians' and 'Muslims') may be seriously challenged. Stable group patterns may be undermined by moral and political disagreements that cut right across religious belonging, or by interreligious solidarity (for instance with victims of hateful speech) which challenges confrontational forms of identity politics on either side.

In Chapters 2 and 3, examples have been given of how some forms of interreligious dialogue in Norway have transcended static forms of group thinking commonly associated with the multiculturalist paradigm, for instance in a joint defence of those who choose to change their religion. Those involved in such dialogues are, anyway, faced with challenges and stories from the others *as individuals*, and there is not always a fixated 'group script' available.

Group interest is still a fact to be dealt with, both by the government's politics of religion, and in interreligious dialogue. In the Norwegian context, the tension between group rights and individual rights has been hard to handle interreligiously. Whereas groups rights are focused on religious freedom, individual rights are typically oriented towards notions of justice (for instance, gender justice) on the basis of which the individual might also want to challenge the established practices of their own religious community – for instance, regarding equal representation on a governing board or (more radically) equal access to religious offices.

In the Nordic countries, where gender equality and gay rights are considered to be strong values defended by legislation, the discussion about group rights and individual rights has crystallized in a heated debate on possible exemptions from the general rule of non-discrimination between the sexes and between people of different sexual orientations in the Gender Equality Act and the Working Environment Act. Here, the religious communities in Norway – supported by the Humanist Association – have in general defended the faith communities' right to differential treatment of men and women, of heterosexuals and homosexuals (Leirvik 2012: 217–20).

Does that reflect a lack of interest in the rights of women and homosexuals or, rather, a shared commitment to a liberal, multicultural society that restricts the ambition of the state to regulate everything? I would rather suggest that the interfaith consensus primarily reflects a dominant concern for the minority rights of faith communities in a Christian majority society which continues to be supported by a (modified) state church system.

The outcome of this discussion in the Norwegian context has been revised versions in the Gender Equality Act and Working Environment Act, on the basis of which the faith communities are allowed to practise differential treatment with regard to central religious offices, but not necessarily in the case of other types of hired personnel. The logic of the present legislation is that the faith communities, in instances of controversy, will have to argue their case vis-à-vis the authorities.

Behind the controversy also lurks the system of financial support for the faith communities from municipal and state budgets, a support which in the Norwegian context is relatively comprehensive. Should the government stipulate certain terms (for instance, regarding gender equality) for such support?[3]

The issue of gender equality, however, is not only a question between the faith communities on the one hand and the state on the other. The struggle for equality and power is also fought *within* the faith communities, for instance with regard to women's access to priesthood in the Catholic Church or to governing bodies in mosques. Whether the state decides to intervene or stay completely neutral in such internal affairs, it influences – for better or worse, depending on the eye of the beholder – the internal power constellations of the religious communities.

If the state chooses to conduct an active, value-based policy vis-à-vis the faith communities – for instance regarding gender equality – the question also arises whether the authorities may find groups within and across the faith communities that have a similar agenda for change. In that case, the state will have to choose between openly competing interests in the religious field and cannot withdraw in the disguise of religious freedom. For whose freedom should trump here?

Interreligious dialogue and liberation theology: The religious and the suffering Other

In theological terms, the tension between faith-based diplomacy and militancy for peace, or that between static multiculturalism and interreligious activism oriented towards change, touches on that between interreligious dialogue and liberation theology (Leirvik 2004b). In his book *One Earth Many Religions* (1995) which carries the subtitle 'Multifaith Dialogue and Global Responsibility', Paul Knitter has attempted a synthesis between the two approaches to religious and social differences. Knitter sees the encounter with the Other as a shattering contrast-experience of facing 'the *really different*, the unexpected, the unthought-of, the surprising, the jolting. I'm talking about people or events that didn't seem to fit into the world that I had experienced or understood' (1995: 1). In this connection, he distinguishes between the 'religious' and the 'suffering' Other.

Knitter's odyssey began with an encounter with 'the religious Other' which led him – as a Jesuit missionary – to recognize that other religious traditions were imbued with a wisdom that both challenged and enriched him. Only through his subsequent solidarity work for refugees and illegal immigrants from Central America to the United States, he explains, he was led to a shattering encounter with 'the suffering Other'. In his book, Knitter also tells the story of an ecological revival that led him to the fundamental recognition of living on a wounded Mother Earth.

For Knitter, so he explains, 'the suffering Other' came to shatter his life far more than the 'the religious Other'. Knitter is adamant that, if forced to choose between 'pluralism' or 'liberation', that is between interfaith dialogue or the struggle for social justice, he would have to abandon dialogue and give priority to the alleviation of suffering and the struggle for justice (1995: 11). But luckily, he says, experiences from interfaith dialogue in Sri Lanka (as described in the book's final chapter) have demonstrated that there is a socially committed, truly liberating form of interfaith dialogue.

The urgent question for everyone committed to both interfaith dialogue and liberation theology must, then, be how to unite a *radical* struggle for justice (led by 'militants for peace'?) that will always be controversial and create conflict with a *liberal* engagement for multi-religious coexistence (facilitated by 'faith-based diplomats'?) in which respect of different opinions must be the cornerstone. How can one, in shifting contexts, reconcile a double responsibility for the religiously Other and the suffering Other?

In some cases, the religious Other may be seen as identical with the suffering Other. In an article from 1996 titled 'The Hidden God. The Divine Other of Liberation', David Tracy speaks about the shocking encounter with an Other who is not only religiously different but also socially and politically marginalized – by an injustice that often coincides with cultural and religious barriers. The doubly Other, says Tracy (reminiscent of Levinas), carries the trace of a hidden God before whom I am absolutely responsible.

But social contractions do not always coincide with religious borders. If one looks more closely into the matter, one will find that social and ideological differences are generally more conspicuous *within* the religions than *between* them.

Transreligious solidarity: A South-African example

On the Muslim side, a challenging reflection on the relation between the religious Other and the suffering Other can be found in the writings of the South African thinker Farid Esack. Esack is a profiled liberation theologian, and a pronounced spokesman for religious pluralism. His most well-known book carries the title *Qur'an, Liberation and Pluralism. An Islamic Perspective of Interreligious Solidarity against Oppression* (1997). The book is written against the background of his experiences from the struggle against apartheid. The author stood side by side with black Christian leaders, was imprisoned with them, and experienced the liberation together with them. (After the liberation, Esack was engaged in governmental work for gender equality and also committed himself – as a civil society activist – to the HIV/AIDS-problem in South Africa.) In his book, he describes the shared (although not identical) experience of 'black' Christians and 'Asian' Muslims, their common struggle, and their shared hopes. The experiences he made challenged him to re-read what the Qur'an says about other believers, and to call for a contextually conscious hermeneutics of the Qur'an. In his book, Farid Esack demonstrates that the passages of the Qur'an that are most confrontational with regard to

Jews and Christians, reflect social contradictions rather than religious ones. The 'unbelievers', he argues, are not those with other articles of faith but, rather, those who – across religious divides – keep people down and are not willing to submit themselves to the one God in a community based on 'oneness' and quality.

In the South-African context, Farid Esack has experienced that religious divides did *not* in any way coincide with the fault lines of injustice and oppression. The point of departure of his contextual theology is the experience of *some* Muslims and *some* Christians who joined hands not only against other Christians (the white majority) but also against the many Muslims who lived relatively comfortably with the apartheid regime because they were 'Asians' and thus more privileged than the blacks. His experience coincides with that of many others, namely that the defining differences do not fall between the faith communities but, rather, between rich and poor, oppressor and oppressed, man and woman in all societies and thus also in every faith community. Enlightened by such experiences, it is possible to read the Qur'an in a different way. For instance, Esack understands the term *islam* (submission) not as the name of a separate religious community but rather as a fundamental attitude, which creates community and makes a difference right across religious divides. He gives the same open-ended interpretation to the Islamic key term of *iman*, faith. According to Esack, true faith is directed towards a God who is greater than all the lords of this world. As such, it may inspire controversial, transreligious alliances for liberation.

Who is allied with whom, then, varies with context. For instance, in October 2002, Indian Christians and Muslims in Tamil Nadu joined hands in demonstrations against a ban on conversion that the Hindu nationalists were able to pass. In the Indian context, the question of changing one's religion has been closely associated with social tensions and the debate over the secular or Hindu-religious nature of the Indian nation state. Historically, there have been many examples of 'untouchables' who – frustrated by a caste system that they have associated with Hinduism – have been drawn to the more egalitarian ideas which they, in contrast, have found with Christians, Muslims and Buddhists.

Whereas, in the Indian context, Christians and Muslims have common interests in defending the right to change one's religion, the situation in many Muslim majority societies is different. Here, Muslim authorities – or Muslim neighbours – often strike back hard against those who convert from Islam to Christianity, using the traditional ban on conversion in Sharia as a weapon to maintain social and political hegemony.

Another variable is ethnicity. In the Sudan, the dominant conflict has seemingly been one between Muslims in the north and Christians and traditional practitioners in the south – culminating in the division between Sudan and South Sudan in 2011. A closer look, however, shows that the ethnic component is just as decisive as the religious one. The war in Darfur was fought between groups of Sudanese Muslims, with different ethnic allegiances. In the north/south conflict, there have been examples of Muslims in the south siding with Christian southerners, and some African Muslims in other countries may have been more sympathetic to the Christian Africans in the south than to their Arab co-religionists in the north. For instance, when a group of Sudanese church leaders visited Norway in 2000, the National Contact Group for Christians and Muslims in Norway facilitated a meeting with the president of the Islamic Council. The then president was a West African who made no secret of his sympathy with the black African cause of the Christians.

If one is surprised by interreligious alliances of this kind, the reason is probably that one has fallen victim to a mounting discourse of identity politics which makes people around the globe believe that 'religion' is the most defining factor in their personal or collective identity. In the real world, age, gender, class, ethnicity and culture may be just as determining elements – as components of identities that are more often than not plural in nature. The fact that individual identities are complex implies also that one may feel affiliated to more than one group. This means that only in a critical awareness of shifting contexts, complex identities and 'impure' alliances can one speak meaningfully about interfaith dialogue, whether in an individual or communal perspective.

6

Tolerance, Conscience and Solidarity: Globalized Concepts in Ethical and Religious Education?[1]

As indicated in previous chapters, the issue of religious and ethical education in school has created much conflict in the Norwegian context but also inspired new visions of dialogical learning. Visions as well as conflicts around religion in school are recognizable across different contexts, and part of a globalized discourse.

Globalization has many arenas and takes manifold expressions. In all arenas of globalization, certain loaded concepts seem to flow freely between the cultures. Notions such as tolerance, freedom and democracy do not fall from heaven. Behind globalized concepts, there are human agents with an agenda of change. But once established, concepts can make a difference on their own, in people's minds and in the real world (cf. Koselleck 1985).

This chapter deals with the relevance of the concepts tolerance, conscience and solidarity for ethical and religious education in school. I will try to show how these concepts – if seen as a whole – may unite the personal, relational and political dimensions of value education. Although the scope of the discussion is global, special attention will be paid to the Palestinian (in the prelude) and (particularly) Egyptian contexts. Both countries are Muslim majority societies in which a globalized discourse on tolerance education competes with the long-standing legacy of confessional religious education (for a broader discussion related also to other Muslim majority countries, see Kaymakcan and Leirvik 2007).

Palestinian Prelude

During a visit to Israel and Palestine in 2005, I picked up the latest issue of 'This Week in Palestine'. My eyes fell on a short reflection entitled 'Knowing Thy Neighbour?' written by Nadia Najjab of the Department of Education and Psychology in Birzeit University, Palestine (2005). Najjab relates a conversation with her 6-year-old daughter Nadine who questions why she and her schoolmate Koreen must go to different religion classes (as in many other countries in the Middle East, Islamic and Christian education are offered as alternative options in public schools). 'I wanted for us to be together in one class', Nadine declares. Najjab also notes that her 8-year-old daughter Leen has become more alert to religious differences and started asking people around her: 'Are you a Christian or a Muslim?'

Asking other parents about their experiences, Najjab's impression is confirmed that Palestinian children are, more than before, looking for religious identity as a basis of distinction. Najjab describes this as a new development in Palestine, which is home to 'a long tradition of sharing the national struggle under a common identity'. In line with this heritage, children may also react with surprise to the fact that religion is in fact treated as a dividing factor in school.

The separation of pupils according to religious affiliation is not at all specific for Palestine. On the contrary, confessional religious education is almost the global rule, with relatively few exceptions of religion and ethics being taught as an inclusive subject in school (as it has been attempted in England, the Scandinavian countries and South Africa).

In Palestine, the potentially divisive effect of confessional religious instruction in school has been countered by the Palestinian Authority's development of inclusive curricula for civic and national education. Within a wider perspective, the region's paramount challenge is that of tolerance education across the Palestinian-Israeli divide – a challenge that probably requires revised curricula for civic education, history teaching and religious education on either side. In her above-mentioned reflection, Nadia Najjab calls for educational programmes that advocate 'the eradication of misconceptions and stereotypes'. Although the Palestinian-Israeli challenge has got some distinctive features in this respect, the educational task of overcoming religious stereotypes is certainly global in nature.

In the Middle East and other places, tolerance education is hampered or even blocked by the reinforced tendency of mobilizing people politically on the basis of religious affiliation – a phenomenon that Amin Maalouf has characterized as a potentially 'murderous' form of identity politics (2000).[2] Parallel to the development of confrontational forms of identity politics in the recent two decades, however, the discourse of tolerance education has also become globalized and may thus represent a potential antidote to divisive trends in religion and politics. In the following, I shall analyse the emerging discourse of 'teaching for tolerance' and discuss whether a social conscience and a sense of group-transcending solidarity can be fostered in school – as a counter to divisive identity politics.

About concepts

Since this chapter deals with globalized concepts, a theoretical clarification of what is meant by 'concept' is in place. A concept (or notion) is more than a word. According to the German historian Reinhart Koselleck, the difference between word and concept becomes clear when historical context is taken into account. A word becomes a concept 'when the plenitude of a politico-social context of meaning and experience in and for which a word is used can be condensed into one word' (Koselleck 1985: 5). An underlying assumption of the following discussion is that the scope and context of such concepts as tolerance, conscience and solidarity has increasingly become that of the global community.

In the analytical framework of conceptual history, as developed by Koselleck in his *Futures Past. On the Semantics of Historical Time* (1985), concepts should not only be seen in retrospect as historical products of the human mind. Once introduced, concepts may become a formative part of history. In this sense, concepts can be powerful. Concepts also tend to live their own life, more or less independently of their origin. This implies that the meaning of globalized concepts is flexible and liable to constant renegotiation – in interaction with social history and the global constellations of power.

Tolerance

In global discussions about value education the notion of tolerance has become a central point of reference, as expressed in UNESCO's 'Declaration of Principles on Tolerance' from 1995.[3] UNESCO's Declaration refers to tolerance as a political and legal requirement as well as a moral duty that must be fostered by knowledge; that is through education. In the Universal Declaration of Human Rights from 1948, promotion of tolerance was already referred to as a central task of education: 'Education . . . shall promote understanding, tolerance and friendship among all nations, racial or religious groups, and shall further the activities of the United Nations for the maintenance of peace' (Article 26.2).

The project 'Teaching for Tolerance', initiated by the Oslo Coalition on Freedom of Religion or Belief, is another example of using tolerance as a keyword in circles concerned with multicultural and interfaith education.[4] As for Egypt (to be further discussed below), the modern Arabic word for tolerance – *tasamuh* – figured prominently in the country's revised curricula for ethical and religious education from the early 2000s.

Although the notion of tolerance has become a cross-cultural point of reference, it is not likely that those who profess tolerance understand it in the same way. The exact implication of globalized concepts is always contested and popular concepts easily become absorbed in political rhetoric.

Tolerance as a politicized concept

In the political realm, 'tolerance' has become one of those values that everyone with an ambition of being politically correct in the new world order would be expected to profess – along with 'freedom', 'human rights' and 'democracy'. Everybody seems also to boast of tolerance as a pivotal value in his or her own culture or religion. For instance, in a fatwa on 'Spirit of Tolerance in Islam', the American Muslim leader Muzammil Siddiqui refers to tolerance as a typically Muslim virtue: 'Muslims have been generally very tolerant people.'[5] And in a gathering with Muslim leaders in the White House in 2002 President George W. Bush pointed to tolerance as 'one of the deepest commitments of America' and a value to be defended, along with 'progress' and 'pluralism', by the war on terrorism.[6]

With regard to the *contested* nature of tolerance, a strategy document from 2003 about US policies vis-à-vis Islamic movements is an interesting case in point. The document 'Civil Democratic Islam', which was produced by the Rand Corporation's National Security Research Division, warns against a too-liberal use of the notion of tolerance that could actually threaten American interest. At a time when 'aggressive voices from the Islamic camp are challenging concepts basic to our civilization, such as the universality of human rights', the document says, 'suspending basic modern values in the hopes of inviting a reciprocal tolerance is a risky approach that merely embolden the opponent' (Benard 2003: 36). On the other hand, the document recommends strategic support for named Islamic intellectuals of modernist/liberal inclination such as Khaled Abou El Fadl,[7] Muhammad Shahrur, Fethullah Gulen and Bassam Tibi (2003: 38f.). The cited intellectuals will probably have mixed feelings about their proposed enrolment in US tolerance policies.

The fact that the notion of tolerance is subject to diverse interpretations, however, does not mean that the notion itself is not useful. On the contrary, the contested nature of tolerance indicates that the concept itself has in fact become a common point of reference in the global community.

The conceptual history of tolerance

Although political ideals and personal virtues associated with tolerance can certainly be identified in pre-modern periods, the *word* tolerance is distinctively modern. Originally referring to the capacity of enduring pain and hardship, tolerance in the sense of being 'patient with or indulgent to the opinions or practices of others' can only be documented in English usage from the eighteenth century onwards.[8] Historically, the concept of tolerance was shaped at a particular point in European history – as a critical response to religious wars and political oppression. As Enrique Dussel notes, 'tolerance was advocated by the Enlightenment in the context of the political discussion over religious freedom, and as an affirmation of the subjective rights of the citizen' (2004: 328).

In the case of John Locke, the term used in the English version of his late seventeenth-century treaty is toleration ('A Letter Concerning Toleration', 1689).[9] Whereas *toleration* is entirely a behavioural term and often associated with politics, *tolerance* is more often seen as a personal virtue or character trait – cf. the expression 'a tolerant person' (Newman 1982: 5).

But, also, the word tolerance can be given either a thin or a thick description. In political thought, tolerance is sometimes watered down to mere toleration of cultural and religious differences. The danger of thin descriptions is that tolerance (when understood only as political toleration) may in fact mean indifference to the other. Out of political necessity, you may be ready to tolerate the other but you do not necessarily care about your neighbour who belongs to a different social or religious group from your own. The UNESCO declaration gives a much thicker definition and refers to tolerance as both a political requirement and a 'moral duty'. In UNESCO's version, tolerance connotes nothing less than 'respect, acceptance and appreciation of the rich diversity of our world's cultures'.

This understanding of tolerance corresponds well to words that have been chosen for tolerance in some other languages – such as the Turkish *hoşgörü* which is composed of a Persian loanword for 'nice' (*hoş*) and a Turkish word for 'sight, vision' (*görüm*). In this interpretation, tolerance means seeing the other in the best way.

The Arabic word for tolerance, *tasamuh*, carries rich classical connotations of personal virtues such as patience and generosity.[10] The coining of *tasamuh* as a word for political tolerance, however, is modern and seems not to have happened until the twentieth century. A liberal understanding of political *tasamuh* can be found in the large Muslim network Nahdlatul Ulama in Indonesia. In their understanding, *tasamuh* has been associated with *tawassut*, 'moderation', and *tawazun*, 'balance' and supposed to express itself in honouring indigenous cultures, showing flexibility towards change, and respecting humanity.[11]

It is not always clear, however, whether *tasamuh* transcends the traditional limits set by Muslim cultures for moral and religious plurality. In the East and West, this question is often blurred when tolerance is praised: exactly where are the implicit limits to tolerance being drawn?

Teaching for tolerance

In educational contexts, both the personal and political dimensions of tolerance should be brought to bear – with a critical awareness of the interrelation between globalized concepts, group interest and political power.

In order to avoid a superficial understanding of tolerance as a more or less unwilling 'toleration' of others, I suggest that teaching for tolerance should be linked with educational efforts at strengthening the bond of *conscience* across cultural and religious divides. This is in line with UNESCO's Declaration of Principles of Tolerance, which (as we have seen) relates tolerance to friendship and (freedom of) conscience.

It seems in fact that young people intuitively link the notion of tolerance with personal qualities and the voice of conscience. When the Oslo Coalition on Freedom of Religion or Belief called for a worldwide writing contest for youth and students, nearly all of the 'Stories of Tolerance' that were submitted associated tolerance with personal relationships, like a bond of conscience across all barriers (Plesner 2004). The winning story portrays a Christian and a Muslim student who were able to reconcile with each other and deepen their friendship – after having been divided for some time over religious differences that were hard to tackle.

Conscience

This understanding of tolerance is in line with UNESCO's Declaration, which (as we have seen) relates tolerance to friendship and (freedom of) conscience.

Although etymologically, the *word* conscience has got Greek and Latin roots, the *concept* of conscience should not be referred to as a European or Christian notion. During the twentieth century the concept of conscience has become thoroughly globalized, not least by the Universal Declaration of Human Rights from 1948.

In Western European languages, words for conscience consist of a word for 'knowing' (the implied meaning of which is moral knowledge) and the prefix 'with'. Thus the English word *con-science* corresponds to Latin *con-scientia* and Greek *syn-eidesis*. The prefixes *syn-* and *con-* indicate that, etymologically, conscience means knowing 'with' someone. It can be 'with' (by) oneself or 'with' others. The tension between the turn inwards (towards the self) and the orientation outwards (towards the others) appears in fact to be constitutive of conscience as a concept.

The critical question, then, is 'with whom' we know something that is intimate and deep enough to be labelled conscientious knowledge? Does conscience only reflect personal convictions ('knowing by oneself') or communal obligations as well ('knowing with the other')? In the latter case, can conscience create a bond between people of different faiths that is stronger than mere toleration of religious differences? (For the following, see Leirvik 2006a.)

The conceptual history of conscience

As mentioned, the European roots of the notion of conscience can be found in classical Greek philosophy that associated conscience (Greek: *syneidesis* or *synesis*) with the heart. In the conceptual history of conscience, the New Testament has played an even more important part. In the influential passage of Romans 2.14f., which informed Thomas Aquinas' later theory about natural law, Paul describes conscience as transcending the confines of the Christian community. The conscience of the gentiles testifies to a moral knowledge which can be shared by Jews, Christians, Greeks and Romans – reflecting the fact that the divine law is written in the heart of every human being: 'What the law requires is written on their hearts, while their conscience also bears witness and their conflicting thoughts accuse or perhaps excuse them.'

Paul's inclusive understanding has also inspired the modern, universalistic notion of conscience. In modern European philosophy, conscience has most often been seen as an *individual* property – associated either with moral autonomy (as in Kant) or a wider quest for human authenticity (as in Rousseau). In both cases, focus has been on the integrity of the individual. Hegel, on the other hand, insisted on the *social* nature of conscience. He regarded Kant's individualized understanding of conscience as insufficient and claimed instead that conscience is essentially knowing with others: 'it is the social element of self-consciousness . . . it has to do with being recognised by others' (Hegel 1952: V, 150).

In the critical philosophy of Ludwig Feuerbach, a pupil of Hegel, conscience is stripped of its transcendent reference and seen merely as other human beings' imprint on the self: 'Conscience is the alter ego, the other I in I' (Feuerbach 1960b: IX). Feuerbach agrees with Hegel's insistence on the social nature of conscience. Feuerbach thus returns conscience to its perceived etymological origin; namely other-directed knowledge:

> Conscience is 'knowing with'. To such a degree is the imprint of the Other woven into my self-consciousness, my self-image, that even the expression of what is more than anything else my own, my innermost, the conscience, becomes an expression of socialism, communality. (Feuerbach 1960b: IX, 282)

In contrast with other modern philosophers' interest in 'good' consciences that dare to be autonomous, Feuerbach sees conscience basically as 'bad' conscience on behalf of the wounded other: 'My conscience is nothing but an I that puts itself in the place of a wounded You' (Feuerbach 1960a: X, 279f.).

Globalizing the notion of conscience

In the course of the nineteenth and twentieth centuries, the notion of conscience has become globalized. Most languages, including those that lack a classical parallel to the notion of conscience, have coined words for conscience that have become an integral part of vernacular usage. The widespread reference to conscience in everyday usage around the globe is probably one of the best examples one can find of globalization in its conceptual and philosophical mode.

In the process of globalizing the notion of conscience, there were several impulses at work. A major factor was the Universal Declaration of Human Rights from 1948. Similar to tolerance, which was moulded as a concept against the background of religious wars in Europe, the globalization of conscience gained ground after the World Wars of the twentieth century. The Preamble of the Universal Declaration states that 'disregard and contempt for human rights have resulted in barbarous acts which have outraged the conscience of mankind'. In Article 1, the reality of a universal conscience is postulated in more positive terms:

> All human beings are born free and equal in dignity and rights. They are endowed with reason and conscience and should act towards one another in a spirit of brotherhood. (Article 1)

Article 1 refers to conscience as the seat of a moral knowledge that is global in nature and associates it with brotherhood. Here, the reference is clearly to conscience's *social* dimension as a morally binding 'knowing with the other' across cultural and religious divides.

Against the possible suspicion that the reference to conscience was included only because of Western influence, it should be noted that it was in fact a Chinese member of the drafting committee who proposed a reference to conscience. In his view, the Christian or Western notion of conscience paralleled the Confucian notion of *jen*. In Chinese script, *jen* is composed of the signs for 'human being' and 'two'. It can be translated as 'two-man-mindedness' or 'consciousness of one's fellow men' (Lindholm 1992: 93).[12]

The Declaration itself also reflects the modern understanding of conscience as a *personal* property. Whereas the Preamble and Article 1 emphasize the social dimension of conscience, in Article 18 'freedom of conscience' is defined as an inviolable right that rests with the individual:

> Everyone has the right to freedom of thought, conscience and religion; this right includes freedom to change his religion or belief, and freedom, either alone or in community with others and in public or private, to manifest his religion or belief in teaching, practice, worship and observance. (Article 18)

Both dimensions of the notion of conscience – individual 'knowing by oneself' and communal 'knowing with the other'– are thus present in the Universal Declaration of Human Rights.

In the 1940s, there were also other impulses pointing in the direction of a globalized concept of conscience. Besides the Universal Declaration, the most important contribution probably came from Mahatma Gandhi. Gandhi saw belief in God as something deeply personal that transcended the confines of religious communities. In the works of Gandhi, the sanctity of human conscience belongs to a cluster of closely related convictions and conceptions such as the inner voice of God, the Gospel of love, passive resistance, non-violence, democracy and religious inclusivism (Gandhi 1946: 27, 39, 78).

Conscience in Arabic

Modern Arabic words for conscience are *damir* and *wijdan* (cf. the Turkish loanword *vicdan*). In Modern Standard Arabic, the salient word for conscience is *damir*. But it is only from the middle of the nineteenth century onwards that *damir* in the sense of moral consciousness starts occurring in dictionaries (Leirvik 2006a: chapter 5). In classical Arabic, the word *damir* refers to innermost knowledge that is not divulged. By their reference to innermost feelings and thoughts, words like *damir* and *wijdan* emphasize conscience's nature of being an individual property (a property which political tolerance is supposed to protect). But in modern Muslim discourses on conscience, one can also find that *damir* is referred to as the basis of a faith-transcending moral community that potentially unites Muslims, Christians and other people of good will.

In the wake of the Universal Declaration of Human Rights and of Gandhi, three Egyptian authors who were all writing in the 1950s and 1960s contributed to the globalization of conscience by putting the notion of *damir* at the centre of their works on religion, philosophy and ethics. The authors in question are 'Abbas Mahmud al-'Aqqad (1889–1964), Muhammad Kamil Husayn (1901–77) and Khalid Muhammad Khalid (1920–96). In circles committed to Christian-Muslim dialogue, these authors have received much attention for groundbreaking works on Muhammad and Christ that have rightly been regarded as landmarks (Leirvik 2006a: chapters 7–9).

'Abbas Mahmad al-'Aqqad (d. 1964) saw 'the law of love and conscience' (*shari'at al-hubb wa-l-damir*) as a uniting element in the messages of Christ and Muhammad, as unfolded in his biography of Christ (*'Abqariyyat al-masih*, 'The genius of Christ') from 1953. In a typically modern mode, al-'Aqqad called for a *jihad* of conscience against petrified religion and authoritarian forms of moral authority (n.d.: 173; cf. Leirvik 2006a: 103).

Khalid Muhammad Khalid also employed *damir* as a pivotal notion when in 1958 he wrote about 'Muhammad and Christ – together on the road' (Khalid 1986). In 1963, Khalid dedicated a whole book to 'Human conscience on its journey towards its destiny' (1963). Here, he presents loyalty to conscience as the uniting bond in the history of religion and philosophy. The book ends not with Muhammad but with a chapter on Mahatma Gandhi as 'the voice of conscience in our time'. For Khalid, being true to conscience was equal to being an authentic human person. In a universalistic mode, he sought to mobilize *damir* for freedom of conscience, social justice and non-violence – with Christ, Muhammad and Gandhi as inclusive role models.

In Kamil Husayn's novel *City of Wrong. A Friday in Jerusalem*, which was published in Arabic in 1954 and translated into English in 1959, the author approaches the highly sensitive issue of the crucifixion of Christ. Instead of debating whether Christ was in the end crucified or not, Husayn describes the events of Good Friday as a drama of human conscience (*damir*). The implication is that all those who took part in the process against Christ suppressed their inner voice and crucified their consciences: 'When they resolved to crucify him it was a decision to crucify the human conscience and extinguish its light. They considered that reason and religion alike laid upon them obligations that transcended the dictates of conscience' (Hussein 1994: 29). Whereas conscience in al-'Aqqad and Khalid is wedded to an optimistic view of rationality and human progress, Husayn seems thus to be more pessimistic on future's behalf and critically aware of human reason's potential for evil.

Conscience, identity politics and the Golden Rule

Now, that is history. Whereas in the 1950s and 1960s, both Muslims and Christians in Egypt emphasized their shared Egyptian identity, the 1970s saw the emergence of huge revival movements in both Egyptian Islam and Coptic Christianity. In contrast with the previous emphasis on the fellow nationality and common humanity of Muslims and Christians, public discourses in the last decades of the twentieth century have increasingly focused on Coptic and Muslim authenticity respectively.

Similar processes have taken place internationally, reflecting the global growth of religious identity politics that imply that a person is first and foremost Christian, Muslim, Hindu, etc. and only in the second place human. Perhaps indicative of the worldwide impact of identity politics, in present-day usage one will often find that people refer to 'Christian' or 'Muslim' consciences rather than to a shared human one.

This may also affect the way people conceive of the Golden Rule, which could be seen as an empathetic expression of conscience's other-directed aspect. Almost universal in its dissemination, the Golden Rule is found in most religious traditions and expressed either in the negative or positive: 'always treat (not) others as you would (not) like them to treat you.'[13] In Jewish-Christian tradition, it has often been seen in the light of the empathetic injunction to 'love your neighbour as yourself'.[14]

But how should the Golden Rule be interpreted? Is it universal in its range or does it only call for solidarity between adherents of the same faith? The Muslim version of the Golden Rule figures prominently at the beginning of al-Bukhari's hadith collection (in the Book of Faith): 'No one of you will become faithful till he wishes for his brother (*li-'akhihi*) what he likes for himself.' The problem is that in the most widely used English translations of al-Bukhari, a narrowing parenthesis is added: 'till he wishes for his (Muslim) brother what he likes for himself'. Although the implication of the Arabic word for brother (*'akh*) may be debatable, the English translations reflect a communalistic understanding that blocks a more universalistic interpretation of Muhammad's saying. The narrowing translations correspond to identity politics that threaten to make religion only a marker of communal borders (Leirvik 2010b).

In educational contexts the question arises of how to teach tolerance in a way that opens rather than restricts the empathetic application of the Golden Rule. It is not sufficient to teach tolerance in the restricted form of superficial toleration. A thicker description of tolerance implies a willingness to invite people who are socially, culturally or religiously other than me into my conscience, in a bonding process that is empathetic in nature and morally obligating. Inviting others into my conscience does not mean that I will have to accept moral norms and values that may be distinctively other than mine. The bond of conscience is different and goes deeper than moral opinions: it implies the readiness to suffer with and stand up for the other, regardless of whether I agree with him/her or not in moral and political matters.

Teaching for tolerance: The case of Egypt

Since public school is such an important common arena in multicultural societies, the question of how to establish deep-seated tolerance is largely a question of whether school education contributes to opening up consciences or not.

Conscience-based tolerance education may necessitate a revision of prevailing models for ethical and religious education. In some European countries, such as England and Norway, efforts have been made to stimulate interfaith learning in school – by substituting confessional instruction for inclusive forms of ethical and religious education. Revised Turkish curricula for 'Religious Culture and Moral Education' (from 2000 and 2005) have stated similar aims (Kaymakcan 2007: 24ff.). In most Western countries, however, the prevailing model is still confessional.

The same is true of the vast majority of Muslim countries. In Egyptian schools, Islamic and Christian Education has been offered as parallel options since 1907 (for the following, see Leirvik 2004b). The inclusion of Christian education on a par with Islamic education was part of the nationalist project in the first part of the twentieth century, when Muslims and Christians in Egypt fought together against British domination and Western missionary influence. But some would say that the sense of social and political unity has in fact been undermined by a system of religious education that reinforces the citizens' sense of being essentially different – as Muslims and Christians.

A short story by the Egyptian author Naguib Mahfouz, much in the same vein as the reflection by Nadia Najjab cited in the prelude of this chapter, illustrates the conflict between sociopolitical integration and religious separation in Egypt. In *Jannat al-atfal* ('The Children's Garden'), which was published in 1969 as part of the collection *Khammarat al-qitt al-aswad*, Mahfouz shows that children may harbour more inclusive intuitions than their parents (who have learnt to accept the dichotomy of the established structures). In the short story, a Muslim daughter interrogates her father about the religious separation in school between herself and her best friend, the Christian girl Nadia. The daughter says that she and Nadia are always together, in the classroom, in the courtyard, and when they eat. 'But in the religion class, I go to one room and Nadia to another!'

In the course of their conversation, the daughter presents her father with the challenging effects of a 'modern pedagogy' that invites children to ask all sorts of hard questions. Reluctantly, the father gives in to his daughter's inquisitiveness. They discuss similarities and differences between Muslims and Christians, agreeing that God is beyond and above all human difference. The conversation ends with the daughter declaring her desire always to be with Nadia, both here and in the afterlife – and 'even in the religion class!' (Mahfouz 1988).

Revised curricula for Islamic and Christian education in *Egypt* initiated in 1993 were still firmly confessional in character, thus separating Muslims and Christians in religious education. But the parallel subjects of Islamic and Christian education were now expected to promote civic values such as tolerance of the other, human rights and co-citizenship (Kouchok 2007). The question is whether such educational ideals can be put into practice as long as Muslims and Christians are not given the chance to converse about ethics and religion face to face, in the classroom.

Then in 2001–2, Egypt introduced a new and inclusive subject called 'Values and ethics' (*al-qiyam wa-l-akhlaq*), not instead of but in addition to religious education in public schools. In the preparation of the subject, the Ministry of Education established a committee of both Muslims and Christians. Pivotal values to be propounded (for instance by use of stories) were freedom, happiness, peace, solidarity, love, economic awareness, humility – and tolerance (*tasamuh*).[15] Regarding Muslim-Christian coexistence, a lesson about peace in one of the first textbooks to be produced pictured a priest and an imam holding a flag together showing the crescent and the cross (the nationalist symbol of the Wafd party from the beginning of the twentieth century).[16]

However, the introduction of a new subject of values and morals, detached from religious education, soon turned out to be highly controversial in the Egyptian context. Islamists organized a media campaign against the new subject and several Muslim leaders argued that it is neither advisable nor possible to separate moral education from religious instruction. In response to initial criticism that the religions' moral traditions were not explicitly referred to, the Curriculum Centre inserted some references to the Qur'an and the Bible in textbooks for the school year 2002–3.[17]

The inclusive subject proved, however, to be short-lived and was abolished after a couple of years, allegedly because it was unpopular with the general public. In 2010, the Ministry of Education announced plans to reintroduce it,[18] but with the toppling of Mubarak's regime in the Arab Spring, the subject's fate was once more sealed.

As for textbooks used in Islamic and Christian education, they too commend friendly relations between Muslims and Christians. The problem is, rather, how the Jews are depicted. In a Christian Religious Education textbook, a section that has got *tasamuh* as an 'embedded theme' comes close to reproducing anti-Jewish stereotypes. When recounting the speech of the first Christian martyr Stephen, his opponents (who are addressed as 'you' in Acts 7) are referred to as 'the Jews' that 'throughout history had disobeyed the Word of God'.[19]

The problem has been even more acute in books for Islamic education, where stereotyped images of the Jews as inherently deceitful have continued to assert themselves side by side with passages that invite friendship between Muslims and Christians. When recounting the initial conflicts between Muslims and Jews in Medina, a fourth-grade textbook from 2002 concluded:

> The Jews are certainly deceitful. They didn't respect the pacts between them and the Muslims, and they didn't respect the rights of the neighbour. The Muslims, however, keep the pacts and have good relations with their neighbours.[20]

Indicative of the strong interrelation between national and religious issues in Egyptian curricula, a section about the benefits of the month of Ramadan drew a direct line from the first Muslims' historic victory over the idolaters at Badr to Egypt's successful October War against the Jewish state Israel in 1973 (for more examples, see Reiss 2003).[21]

Egyptian textbooks seem to corroborate a sense of value community between Muslims and Christians. They may even be read as strengthening the mutual bond of conscience, more or less in the tradition of the inclusive discourses of *damir* that I have cited from the 1950s and the 1960s. The problem is that the concept of tolerance is severely restricted as long as anti-Jewish tendencies continue to assert themselves in the textbooks. This must, of course, be seen in the light of the current conflict between Arabs and Jews. But it probably also reflects the fact that Jews are not present in Egyptian classrooms, as visible others that might invite empathy in spite of political conflict. It is precisely here that tolerance and conscience will have to stand its test – under the pressure of social and political conflicts, and in contexts where the most disturbing others may not even be present.

Solidarity

In such cases, the question of teaching tolerance and fostering conscience also becomes a matter of solidarity. As a globalized concept, 'solidarity' (in Arabic:

takaful or *tadamun*) is more recent than both tolerance and conscience. The concept of solidarity has to do with 'being perfectly united or at one . . . in interests, sympathies or aspirations'.[22] The word itself is of French origin. Formulated by French revolutionaries in the 1840s, it has most often been used in connection with the labour movement and its unity in struggle. In the Northern European context, the welfare state system has been referred to as the expression of a modern 'solidarity society'. State welfare arrangements such as free education, social security for all and universal health services have to a large extent been brought about by the labour movement but encompass by definition all groups of society and their varying needs. In this process, impulses from Christian Democratic movements and parties have also played an important part (Stjernø 2005).

In the 1980s the concept of solidarity got additional momentum from the independent labour movement *Solidarność* in Poland, which also played an important part in dismantling the iron curtain. And in connection with the emergence of twentieth-century liberation movements in the Third World, the expression 'international solidarity' became a central term for those who sided with a just cause other than their own.

What then is the relation between solidarity and tolerance? In his deconstruction of the concept of tolerance, the theologian and philosopher Enrique Dussel contrasts intolerance not with tolerance but with solidarity (2004). According to Dussel, intolerance needs a more powerful antidote than tolerance in the sense of toleration. A narrow understanding of tolerance may in fact imply indifference to the other, implying that one tolerates the other 'with a certain passivity by means of which one absolves oneself of the other's fate'. Instead, Dussel calls for a tolerance-transcending attitude that is 'positive, creative, and responsible for the other'. This is what solidarity means to Dussel – a responsibility for the other that implies that 'the other is actively and positively respected in his alterity' (2004: 330).

In Dussel's understanding, solidarity is not a matter of group interest. It has to do with group-transcending *sympathy* – which literally means 'suffering with' the other. In Dussel's understanding, moving beyond tolerance does not mean blurring moral differences or neglecting painful social and political conflicts. What solidarity means is readiness to suffer with others, even with enemies – in response to their vulnerability. At a deeper level, solidarity may even imply *loving* the enemy, without giving up the right to resist or confront him.

With reference to the Jewish-Christian-Muslim problematic illustrated above, calling for Muslim-Christian friendship at the cost of Jews clearly contradicts a solidarity that is ready to suffer with the other and to protect vulnerable individuals irrespective of their political and religious affiliation. For the same reasons, conservative alliances between Jews and Christians in the West against radical Muslims could not be called solidarity in Dussel's sense. A faith-transcending solidarity must unmask the excluding nature of identity politics, be it in the form of Muslim-Christian or Christian-Jewish alliances. A call for solidarity in Dussel's sense also invites a critical examination of the unequal power relations that are often blurred in superficial declarations of Muslim-Christian unity, in Egypt or elsewhere. For instance in Norway, Christian-Muslim dialogue constantly runs the risk of veiling the unequal balance between the powerful majority and a vulnerable minority.

Dussel's understanding of solidarity is well in tune with Paul Ricoeur's understanding of conscience as becoming 'oneself as another' (1994). Becoming oneself as another requires empathetic identification with others who may sometimes – when recognized in their alterity and vulnerability – represent a painful difference. As Feuerbach put it: 'My conscience is nothing but an I that puts itself in the place of a wounded You' (Feuerbach 1960a: 279f., my translation).

Drawing and transcending limits to tolerance

I have argued that the critical question to tolerance education is whether school education expands the scope of conscience-based solidarity, or narrows it. But transcending cultural and religious boundaries in conscience-based education may mean simultaneously drawing limits to tolerance at a different level. In UNESCO's Declaration of Principles on Tolerance it is stated: 'the practice of tolerance does not mean toleration of social injustice or the abandonment or weakening of one's convictions'. Against injustice and oppression, intolerance is called for. But when confronting social justice, resisting political oppression and claiming freedom of conscience, boundaries will more often than not be drawn right across cultural and religious divides. The real challenge will then be how to draw necessary limits to tolerance *together*, so that pupils can be trained in confronting injustice and inequality, oppression and violence on an *interfaith* basis.

Teaching *tolerance* implies calling on the pupils' *consciences*, helping them to learn faith-transcending *solidarity*. This understanding implies that individual consciences – when called upon in a multireligious context – may form a new kind of moral community that challenges traditional limits to tolerance set by the religions. If pupils of different faiths and backgrounds recognize each other and develop empathy across religious divides, will they still accept traditional inequalities in rights and opportunities between different religious groups, between believers and unbelievers, between men and women?

If successful, conscience-based tolerance education may gradually lay the ground for interfaith solidarity. But that can probably only happen if pupils are allowed to *face each other* when learning ethics, talking about religion and politics, and discussing tolerance.

7

Interreligious Hermeneutics and the Ethical Critique of the Scriptures[1]

In recent years, interreligious hermeneutics has become a relatively well-established *topos* in theorizing about dialogue between the religions. It varies, however, whether the notion refers to relations between people or between texts, and how the interaction between texts and people (readers) is dealt with hermeneutically. For instance in Catherine Cornille and Christopher Conway's edited book *Interreligious Hermeneutics* (2010), the notion is used in a very broad sense covering 'a variety of critical issues in the area of interreligious understanding and interpretation' (2010: ix). Another book with the same heading focuses a bit more on the interpretation of texts, although in a wider perspective signalled by the subtitle 'between texts and people' (Cheetham et al. 2011).

In this chapter, after some reflections on the complexity of the notion of interreligious hermeneutics, I will focus on *textual* hermeneutics. I will discuss (1) background problems and hermeneutical outlooks in some recent examples of Christian-Muslim readings; (2) the question of sacred texts in new contexts; and (3) the issue of ethical critique – alternatively: moral enrichment – of texts regarded to be holy. This last theme being the main focus of this chapter, I will discuss separately how the question of ethical critique is dealt with by some Christian and Muslim theologians respectively, before raising the question of critical engagement with sacred texts in shared spaces.

Interreligious hermeneutics – between texts and people

According to Martha Frederiks, interreligious hermeneutics can either be focused of 'Interpreting the Texts' or 'Interpreting the Encounter with "The Other"' (2005). In the latter case, interreligious hermeneutics comes close to comparative theology, understood as an interpretive approach to other religions which (differently from what is conventionally understood as 'comparative religion') engages the Self in a potentially transformative encounter with the religious Other. What takes place in such dialogical processes is a repositioning of the self into a larger interpretive whole. In Paul Riceour's hermeneutical language, such processes could also be interpreted as becoming 'oneself as another' (Ricoeur 1994).

An example of how the notion of interreligious hermeneutics may be used in the broader sense can also be found in the theologian Bård Mæland's investigation of what he calls 'the interreligious hermeneutics' and the resultant 'comparative theologies' of Kenneth Cragg and Wilfred Cantwell Smith (Mæland 2003). For both Cragg and Cantwell Smith, their interreligious hermeneutics can only be understood in the context of their living encounter with Islam. The question to be investigated is 'how one's self-understanding is formed, influenced, affected, interrogated, etc.', entailing some kind of 'self-change' brought about by these Christian thinkers' encounter with the Muslim other (Mæland 2003: 4f.).

Also, in the Danish theologian Jonas Adelin Jørgensen's (2009) study of syncretistic Jesus-believers in Asia, the text to be interpreted is not the other but the precarious position of oneself. Jørgensen's research deals with the syncretistic experience of Jesus-believers who posit themselves in the liminal space between Islam and Christianity (*'Isa imandars* – 'those faithful to Jesus' – in Bangladesh) or Hinduism and Christianity (*Khrist Bhaktas* – 'devotees of Christ' – in India). In the way Jørgensen employs the notion of interreligious hermeneutics, it comes close to an inner dialogue of converts who in spite of their dedication to Christ retain several elements of their previous faith and practice (Jørgensen 2008, 2009).

The notion of interreligious hermeneutics may be used in similar ways to characterize what takes place in Christian-Buddhist encounters. In an article about the Japanese Christian theologian S. Yagi and his existential dialogue with Buddhism, Sybille Fritsch-Oppermann (2003) notes that 'a hermeneutics of the Other' (in Levinas' sense) is basically about an understanding of myself as provoked by the other, more than an understanding of the other person or a text belonging to the other. Interreligious hermeneutics has always to do with the understanding of persons, not only of texts (Fritsch-Oppermann 2003: 235f.).

Similarly in Martha Frederiks' understanding, interreligious hermeneutics in the broader sense arises from 'an encounter with the stranger, the other being the text to be interpreted' (2005: 105). What unites interreligious hermeneutics as 'interpreting the texts' and 'interpreting life', according to Frederiks, is the anchoring point in everyday life experiences of people living together in a multireligious society. It is this lived experience that may also lead to shared reflection on the religious scriptures:

> Sometimes borrowing from each others' interpretation frames, but always sharing the hope and encouragement we received from reading the sacred texts; always living, reading, interpreting, making sense of life with the other in heart and mind. (Frederiks 2005: 106)

In the following, I will concentrate on two aspects of what happens when people of different faiths engage in dialogue about sacred texts. First, I will reflect on the different *contexts* in which scriptures may be read interreligiously. Second, I will discuss the question of *ethical critique* of the Holy Scriptures – related to commonly acknowledged problems in particular contexts and the way in which problematic religious practices may be legitimated by reference to sacred scripture.

Background problems in interreligious readings

As indicated by the above quote from Frederiks, interreligious hermeneutics in the sense of reading texts together across religious differences is more often associated with religious 'encouragement' than with moral critique. The most obvious exception would be critical feminist readings, which may also shed critical light on interreligious dialogues about scriptures (cf. Egnell 2011; Grung 2011a). Another equally critical question emerging from interreligious readings regards the image of the religious Other in the Holy Scriptures and its possible function as fuel for violent confrontations.

In which contexts are such critical questions to the scriptures allowed to surface, and how are 'problematic texts' (problematic with regard to gender models, enemy images and violence) dealt with in differing forms of interreligious dialogue?

If a general reluctance to open up for moral critique when discussing interreligious hermeneutics can be observed, this does not imply that dialogues about sacred scripture generally eschew *problems*. When looking at some books from the last decades about Christians and Muslims reading their sacred texts together, one will easily detect that certain problems related to actual uses of scriptures lurk in the background. In the groundbreaking book *The Challenge of the Scriptures*, by a French-North African research group of Christians and Muslims, the background problem is clearly the lack of recognition of the other's scriptures and their integrity among mainstream Christians and Muslims (Group 1989). In *Scriptures in Dialogue*, a book emerging from ongoing Anglican-Muslim dialogue, along with the already-mentioned issue of how the religious Other is depicted in the Bible and the Qur'an, the critical question of gender relations also shines through in the selection of topics and texts (Ipgrave 2004).

Also, in a book from the German context about scriptural interpretation in Christianity and Islam ('*Nähe ist dir das Wort . . .*'), feminist readings are part of the horizon, but here in a more general framework of critical hermeneutics (Schmid, Renz, and Ucar 2010). The problem-oriented and radical-hermeneutical approaches of this particular book shine through in the titles of the Muslim and Christian chapters that deal with feminist readings: 'Gender justice and gender-jihad: Possibilities and limitations of women-liberating interpretations of the Qur'an' and 'The female reader decides! Chances and limitations of feminist interpretive paradigms' (2010: 129ff., my translation). In a Swedish book about interpretation of the Jewish-Christian Bible and the Qur'an (*Att tolka Bibeln och Koranen*), chapters on feminist interpretation do in fact dominate the discussion – here too in the general framework of critical hermeneutics (Stenström 2009).

As for the concept of *Scriptural Reasoning* and its corresponding movement of Jews, Christians and Muslims reading the Holy Scriptures together, its proponents explicitly posit their project as an antidote to schismogenetic processes in general society. The general lack of wisdom-seeking conversation between the children of Abraham, as well as antagonistic discourses in the public sphere, are part of the negative background for the movement's 'mutually critical engagement . . . aimed at transforming the public sphere for the better . . . seeking the public good for the sake of God and God's peaceful purposes' (Ford 2006: 20). The proponents of Scriptural Reasoning do recognize that the way in which Jews, Christians and Muslims use their scriptures may just as well be part of the problem as a potential resource for peaceful coexistence:

> Each of these scriptures has texts that can be used to legitimate violence, claims to superiority, blanket condemnations, cruel punishments, suspicions, oppressive morality, and hostility to those who are not believers of God as identified by one's own tradition. (Ford 2006: 2)

The question still remains of how these insights are dealt with in a critical hermeneutical perspective: are such interpretations referred to only a 'misuses' of religious texts, or may Scriptural Reasoning lead to critical conversation about the scriptures themselves, as literary conveyors of problematic messages?

Sacred texts in new social contexts

The historical background for contemporary concepts of interreligious hermeneutics is the fact that people who by birth belong to different communities of interpretation may create new hermeneutical spaces away from 'home'. This implies that ever-new contexts for scriptural interpretation evolve. Critical questions regarding the basic messages of the scriptures and their actual interpretation may arise both in the respective religious communities and in new contexts where scriptures from different traditions are dealt with in shared spaces.

From a global perspective, sacred scriptures and religious traditions are no longer the exclusive property of their religion of origin and its established authorities. Sacred scriptures have increasingly come to be seen as *world scriptures*, in analogy with world music. The concept of 'world scripture' may be seen as an offshoot of the academic discipline of comparative religion, including its more popular expressions (Wilson 1991), and has also been picked up in a pamphlet by Ursula King (1999) which speaks of the world's scriptures as 'resources for dialogue and renewal'.

In the Norwegian context, a book series entitled 'The World's Sacred Scriptures' (*Verdens Hellige Skrifter*) was launched in 2000. The series soon became a veritable sales success, ever expanding the notion of sacred scripture and comprising a seemingly never-ending chain of volumes. Whether such a wealth of world scriptures is actually read, or merely shelved as a token of cultural capital, is hard to judge. But more than ever before, sacred scriptures *are* read and discussed across traditional boundaries – as personal inspiration or in conversation with others.

As for social contexts of interpretation, the proponents of Scriptural Reasoning speak of interpretative practices carried out in the threefold context of *houses, campuses and tents* respectively (Ford 2006: 7–13).

House stands for home. But people seldom live their entire lives at home. Parallel to the hermeneutical work that is carried out in churches, synagogues and mosques (in the religions' own houses) there is also (especially in Northern Europe) a strong legacy of interpreting the sacred scriptures and exploring the relevance of the religious traditions in *campuses*, that is in the context of the academy. As other religious traditions become rooted in European academia, possibilities also open up for critical and constructive engagement with sacred scriptures on an interreligious, academic basis (cf. Chapter 1).

In connection with David Ford's discussion of campuses as a shared, interpretative space, I would suggest that primary and secondary *schools* should also be considered as a similar context for interreligious hermeneutics. In some countries that have developed inclusive forms of religious education in school, sacred scriptures have even become textbooks in the classroom. Dealing with the Bible and the Qur'an in the classroom is something different from dealing with the Bible *or* the Qur'an in parallel options of Christian or Islamic education. How can sacred texts be dealt with in a classroom where many different traditions (including secular ones) are vividly represented? According to the curriculum for religious education in upper secondary schools in Norway (from 2006) students are expected to learn how to interpret sacred scriptures. What does that imply with regard to established notions of authority which imply that only those who are well-versed in traditional exegesis can interpret the scriptures? How does one approach the issue of interreligious hermeneutics in a situation where everyone may hold instantaneous authority, be it in inspired bids for interpretation in the classroom or in more informal settings?

In addition to what takes place in institutionalized settings of houses and campuses (and schools), believers may occasionally pitch *tents* in the open spaces between the religious traditions. A tent in this sense means a temporary place meant for sharing, for instance by reading each others' sacred scriptures together in dialogue groups. According to David Ford, the metaphor of the tent refers to

> what happens in the *interpretive* space between the three scriptures [of Judaism, Christianity and Islam]; in the *social* space between mosque, church and synagogue; in the *intellectual* space between 'houses' and 'campuses', and between disciplines on the campuses; in the *religious and secular* space between the houses and the various spheres and institutions of society; and in the *spiritual* space between interpreters of scripture and God. (Ford 2006: 12)

As Ford indicates, scriptural and theological reasoning across religious traditions has both a secular and a spiritual dimension to it. As for the spiritual aspect, Martin Buber in his philosophy of dialogue suggests that everything that takes places in the 'realm of between' has the potential of becoming a dwelling place of the Holy Spirit (2002: 240–2).

But the secular dimension of interreligious hermeneutics is equally important. As mentioned, the proponents of scriptural reasoning emphasize that hermeneutical praxis in the spaces between the religions should be *public* in the sense of addressing shared challenges in society.

Ethical critique of sacred texts

Whereas the notion of world scriptures seems to connote inspiration and spiritual enrichment across religious traditions, the concept of scriptural reasoning relates (as noted) more clearly to commonly acknowledged problems with regard to interreligious coexistence in wider society. Some of these problems clearly reflect the way in which the religious Other is depicted (or stereotyped) in the sacred texts themselves. It is not clear, however, whether scriptural reasoning would be open to critical hermeneutics which allow the readers to challenge such parts of the sacred texts on moral and religious grounds.

Where does the notion of ethical critique of scripture come from? Although the notion itself seems to be recent (cf. below), the idea that religion needs to be criticized on moral grounds is of course much older. With regard to the Jewish-Christian tradition, it could be argued that the Bible itself is characterized by a critical dialogue between different scriptures, often with moral issues at the fore (cf. prophetic critique of nationalist religion, as expressed in the books of the Jewish Bible).

As for the European Enlightenment, Immanuel Kant's ethical critique of the story about Abraham and Isaac in light of the moral law could be cited as the beginning of a moral critique of the Bible on modern grounds (Gilje 2009: 69f.; cf. Kant's *Die Religion innerhalb der Grenzen der blossen Vernunft*). In both the Bible and the European Enlightenment, we may also observe how moral critique is essentially a form of self-critique. In this respect, moral critique of the other's texts, as in contemporary Christian or secular critique of the Qur'an, is a totally different project which does not involve any form of self-change.

In twentieth-century critiques of religion, one may observe a general shift from intellectual to moral criticism (before the return of rational critique by the so-called new atheism of Richard Dawkins, Christopher Hitchens and others at the beginning of the twenty-first century). The distinction between intellectual and moral critique is made by the secular humanist Bertrand Russell in his essay 'Has Religion Made Useful Contributions to Civilisation?' from 1930:

> The objections to religion are of two sorts – intellectual and moral. The intellectual is that there is no reason to suppose any religion true; the moral objection is that religious precepts date from a time when men were more cruel than they are, and therefore tend to perpetuate inhumanities which the moral conscience of the age would otherwise outgrow . . . It is not only intellectually, but also morally, that religion is pernicious. (Russell 1967: 31, 28)

In the latter half of the last century, a similar ethical turn can in fact be seen in Christian theology and biblical studies, in its development from historical criticism to biblical hermeneutics focused on the ethics of interpretation. In her presidential address to the Society of Biblical Literature in 1987 Elisabeth Schüssler Fiorenza called for 'a paradigm shift in the ethos and rhetorical practices of biblical scholarship' (Fiorenza 1988: 16). Stressing the political responsibility of biblical scholars with regard to their 'rhetorical' role in the public sphere, she called for an increased awareness of 'the ethics of biblical interpretation' – suggesting that 'raising ethical-political and religious-theological questions' should be seen 'as constitutive of the interpretive process' (1988: 13). She summoned biblical scholars not only to take public responsibility for their choice of interpretive methods but equally 'for the ethical consequences of the biblical text and its meanings' (1988: 15). Developing her argument, she approximated a position that could in fact be called 'ethical critique of the Bible', as she located the ethical problem not only in the act of interpretation but in the authorial construction of the texts themselves:

> If scriptural texts have served not only noble causes but also to legitimate war, to nurture anti-Judaism and misogynism, to justify the exploitation of slavery, and to promote colonial dehumanization, then biblical scholarship must take the responsibility not only to interpret biblical texts in their historical contexts but also to evaluate the construction of their historical worlds and symbolic universes in terms of a religious scale of values. (Fiorenza 1988: 15)

Whereas Russell's moral challenge came from outside of the established interpretive community (similar to Ibn Warraq's sequel *Why I am not a Muslim*, from 1995), Schüssler Fiorenza raises her concern from home. Her critique is voiced from within the Christian 'house' but also from within a 'campus' of university theology which remains (in the West) strongly influenced by the household concerns of Christianity.

Also at the nexus between house and campus, Schüssler Fiorenza's challenge from 1988 has been taken up by feminist theologians and by biblical scholars who have called for a 'moral' or 'ethical' critique of the language of dominance and violence in the Bible. Michael Prior's book *The Bible and Colonialism* (from 1997) as well as his article 'Ethical Cleansing and the Bible' (from 2002) are furnished with the subtitle 'A Moral Critique' (1997, 2002). Prior's project is to examine the legitimating function biblical texts have had for colonial politics in Latin America, South Africa and Palestine.

According to Prior, these case studies 'highlight some of the moral problems at the heart of the Bible itself . . . several traditions within the Bible lend themselves to oppressive interpretations and applications precisely because of their inherently oppressive nature' (2002: 46).

In the Nordic context, several biblical scholars have taken up the impulses from Michael Prior and pursued his concern in a wider thematic framework. For instance, the Norwegian New Testament scholar Halvor Moxnes has discussed Palestinian and homosexual minority concerns in relation to critical biblical texts and their dominant interpretation (1999).

Impulses from both Schüssler Fiorenza and Prior were taken up by the Finnish New Testament scholar Heikki Räisänen who has also published widely in the field of (inter)religious studies. When, in a lecture in Uppsala in 1999, he called for 'an ethical critique' of the Bible (Räisänen 2000), his call should be seen in the light of an earlier collection of essays entitled *Marcion, Muhammad and the Mahatma* (Räisänen 1997). In this book, Räisänen sets out to demonstrate how Marcion and his rejection of the Old Testament, Muhammad and the Qur'an, Joseph Smith and the Book of Mormon and Mahatma Gandhi's eclectic reading of the Gospels could all be seen as examples of intended 'improvements' on the Hebrew and/or Christian Bible. As for ethical critique, Räisänen underlines the strong moral indignation in Marcion's biblical exegesis and suggests that his reaction to the alleged violence of Old Testament 'resembles the reaction of radical feminist interpreters to a Bible experienced as a hopelessly patriarchal book' (Räisänen 1997: 69; cf. Räisänen 2000).

In his call for an ethical critique of the Bible, Räisänen adds a professional concern for the exegete's responsibility for 'confronting the texts with our ethical values' (2000: 239). In his ten commandments for ethical critique, Räisänen realizes that no universal agreement on ethical principles (by which to confront the texts) can be presupposed, and that the question of 'whose values' needs always to be asked. He nevertheless refers to general values such as 'love, justice and humanity' in his call for a confrontation of all kinds of violence, physical as well as symbolic, in the biblical texts (2000: 240, 242).

Picking up Räisänen's concern for an ethical critique, the Swedish New Testament scholar Hanna Stenström criticizes Räisänen for being too vague in defining the values upon which an ethical critique should be based. Informed by postmodern and power-critical sensibilities, she calls for transparency in the choice of values and also stresses the need to combine ethical critique with political critique of dominant ideologies – not least gendered ones (Stenström 2001, 2002).

The cited examples are all related to Western contexts, the interpretive tradition of Christianity, and a university theology still conducted within a largely Christian horizon. The question is how ethical critique of the scriptures can be dealt with in theological faculties bent on widening their scope to other traditions and developing different forms of interreligious studies.

In my own 'campus', the University of Oslo's Faculty of Theology, new courses within the field of interreligious studies have also approached the issues of interreligious hermeneutics and ethical critique of sacred scriptures. Examples of course titles would be 'Problematic biblical texts', 'Interreligious hermeneutics: interpretation of the Bible and the Qur'an' and 'Modern critique of religion'. As the Faculty has gradually become more multireligious with regard to the student body, these courses have sought to create an interreligious space for struggling with the hermeneutical issue of moral or ethical critique – in a shared, academic space. Similar developments could be cited from many other theological faculties.

Moral critique or moral enrichment? Some Muslim perspectives

How has the question of moral critique been dealt with by Muslim academics?

In responding to internal and external calls for a moral critique of texts and their interpretations, several examples of intellectual convergence with Christian counterparts can be cited – for instance in the way Muslim feminist theologians have critically elaborated on Christian feminist approaches to the scriptures (Roald 1998). As Anne Sofie Roald has demonstrated (2011), issues related to gender models and the position of women in family, faith communities and society are often the triggering factors for new interpretive approaches to sacred scriptures among Muslims in Europe. These are of course common challenges for, for example, Christians and Muslims, although the hermeneutical responses vary both between and within the two interpretive communities.

In current discussions, at least in the West, criticism of gender inequality, discrimination against religious minorities and religiously inspired violence is typically articulated as a critique of the qur'anic message itself; that is not merely as question of how religious texts can be 'misused'. Whereas the discourse of misuse seems to be the dominant one among Muslim believers, critique of the sacred text is most often launched from outside of the interpretive community – by self-proclaimed apostates (cf. Ibn Warraq's *Why I am not a Muslim*, 1995), representatives of the New Christian Right (cf. Mark Gabriel's *What the Quran Really Teaches About Christianity, Violence and the Goals of the Islamic Jihad*, 2002), or neoconservative critics of Islam (cf. Geert Wilders' film *Fitna*, 2008).

A controversial voice is the Canadian lesbian author Irshad Manji, who in her book *The Trouble with Islam* (2003) criticizes dominant views of sexuality, authoritarian blocking of critical questions and anti-Jewish attitudes in Muslim circles. Insisting (like Amina Wadud and other Islamic feminists) that different interpretations of the Qur'an are possible, Manji takes a step further by suggesting that the Qur'an itself might not be entirely 'perfect':

> The Koran is not transparently egalitarian for women. It's not transparently anything except enigmatic . . . Far from being perfect, the Koran is so profoundly at war with itself that Muslims who 'live by the book' have no choice but to choose what to emphasize and what to downplay. (Manji 2003: 39f.)

Declared as an apostate by some, Manji herself insists of being heard as a critical voice from within the interpretive community of Muslims. Manji's own message is hermeneutically quite simple: stop pretending that decisions made on the basis of the Qur'an are dictated by God – they are made by 'free human will' (2003: 39).

Some Muslim academics have responded to calls for a moral critique of the scriptures by developing their own, congenial approaches to qur'anic hermeneutics. Egyptian-American Khaled Abou El Fadl is an interesting example. When criticizing authoritarian structures, gender inequality (*Speaking in God's Name. Islamic Law, Authority, and Women*, 2001) and intolerance of other faiths (*The Place of Tolerance in Islam*, 2002), Abou El

Fadl criticizes of course the interpretive tradition but also opens up for a critical, dialogical hermeneutics of the Qur'an. As for interreligious relations, he admits that Islamic puritans or militant Islamists may in fact muster 'a set of textual references in support of their exclusionary and intolerant theological orientation' (Abou El Fadl et al. 2002: 11). Abou El Fadl does not, however, speak of an ethical critique of the sacred text but introduces instead the notion of moral enrichment. Noting that the Qur'an repeatedly appeals to the moral sense of its reader, by use of general terms such as 'justice' of the Arabic notion of *al-ma'ruf* (what is commonly known to be good), he suggests that

> the Qur'anic text assumes that readers will bring a preexisting, innate moral sense to the text. Hence the text will morally enrich the reader, but only if the reader will morally enrich the text. The meaning of the religious text is not fixed simply by the literal meaning of its words, but depends, too, on the moral construction given to it by the reader. (Abou El Fadl et al. 2002: 15)

A similar approach is developed by Ebrahim Moosa in a chapter about 'The debts and burdens of critical Islam' in the anthology *Progressive Muslims. On Justice, Gender, and Pluralism* (2002). In his view, 'critical Islam' will have to abandon apologetic responses to legitimate criticism, since 'the false utopias of ideal and perfect Muslim societies in the past, widely touted by ideologues of authoritarianism, will not survive the scrutiny of history' anyway (Moosa 2002: 117). He also notes that a number of practices seemingly sanctioned by the normative sources have in fact been abandoned by modern Muslim sensibilities: 'For a whole set of reasons, we no longer consider marriage to what our modern culture deems minors, corporeal punishment, and the death penalty to be acceptable practices' (2002: 122). Like Abou El Fadl, Moosa takes a step further from historical critique towards a critical conversation with the sacred text itself by suggesting that all kinds of 'text fundamentalism' must be avoided and the critical response of the reader must be taken seriously – even in 'in the process of revelation'. Referring to indisputable patriarchal features of the Qur'an, he writes:

> It may be preferable to hear the Qur'an in its patriarchal voice but to understand it with the sensibility of an actor/reader/listener/reciter immersed in the process of revelation. It is that listener/reciter who discovers through her or his history, experience, and transformed inner sensibility that gender justice, equality, and fairness is a norm for our time, and not patriarchy. (Moosa 2002: 125)

What shines through in Moosa's reasoning, is an *ethical* hermeneutics focused on the reader's response. Involving the reader in the very process of revelation, he formulates even a *theological* hermeneutics characterized by interactivity. Criticizing those who exclusively seek authority in some founding text for failing 'to engage the text in an interactive manner', he claims that

> It is precisely such interactivity that transforms the human being who is ultimately the subject of revelation, and who has to embody the qualities that combat patriarchy and endorse justice and equality . . . The truth is that we 'make' the norms in conversation with the revelatory text. (Moosa 2002: 125)

Critical engagement with sacred texts – in shared spaces?

The cited examples of how to deal with ethical conflicts in the encounter between sacred texts and contemporary readers are related to internal processes among (Scandinavian) Christian and (US-based) Muslim theologians. Cross-religious challenges may still be implicated when theologians discuss the relation between ethics and hermeneutics at home (in their respective 'houses'), especially when such reflections are articulated in the shared space of the university's increasingly pluralistic 'campuses'.

In tent-like forums for interreligious dialogue, reading sacred scriptures together has increasingly become part of the agenda. Although such attempts (as described above) may often be problem-related, few examples can be cited of how for instance Christians and Muslims engage together in a critical dialogue not only about but also with the sacred texts – as a joint interpretive community. One example might be Anne Hege Grung's study of what takes place when Christian and Muslim women sit down together trying to make meaning of (from women's point of view) problematic texts from the Bible, the Qur'an and Hadith (2011a).

Scriptural reasoning's metaphor 'tent' signals the provisional character of such attempts. Can one also foresee the formation of more stable interreligious, interpretive communities away from home? Critical engagement with sacred scriptures in the context of universities (university theology rather than religious studies) is perhaps the most promising possibility. But in countries that have developed common subjects of religious education in primary and secondary schools (such as in England and Scandinavia), the phenomenon of interreligious interpretive communities (here, on a non-scholarly basis) may also take place in the classroom. As cited above, the curriculum for the subject 'Religion and Ethics' in upper secondary school in Norway presupposes that the student will learn to interpret sacred scriptures in an increasingly multireligious setting where critical approaches to religious traditions are likely to be heard on a regular basis. The same may happen in lower secondary schools (in the corresponding subject 'Religion, Life Stances and Ethics') if the curriculum's reference to modern critique of religion is related (by textbooks, teachers and/or students) to sacred traditions.

To prepare teachers for such scenarios, a Norwegian textbook about narrative pedagogy meant for teacher training in religion includes chapters on 'stories in conflict' (parallel and conflicting stories about Jesus, etc.) and 'challenging stories'. The latter chapter discusses how to handle stories from the great traditions that are felt to be problematic with regard to gender models, ethical sensibilities (particularly in relation to idealized violence in the texts) and brutalized images of God (Breidlid and Nicolaisen 2011: 407–46).

Whereas Breidlid and Nicolaisen, in their didactical reflections, tackle the question of problematic texts head on, a collection of religious source texts prepared for religious education in Norwegian schools seems rather to avoid the problem. For instance, under the headings of 'religious tolerance' and 'war and peace' in Islam, the resource book selects only (sections of) qur'anic verses that would seem to support a tolerant and peaceful interpretation, simply ignoring more problematic passages in the same literary contexts (Rasmussen and Thomassen 1999: 268; cf. my critique in Leirvik 1999). On the contrary, a more recent textbook for religious education in lower secondary school tackles problematic texts from the Bible and the Qur'an (regarding gender issues, interreligious relations, enemy images, war and peace) quite openly. One section has actually got the heading 'Critique of religious models and sacred scriptures in the religions' (Holth and Kallevik 2008: 113–27).

What may come out of such critical conversations in the classroom is hard to judge. In the long term, it *could* contribute to creating an interreligious dialogue in general society that is not vilifying this or that tradition over against the other but instead treats the problem of an ethical reading of sacred texts as a *shared* challenge.

Towards shared hermeneutical approaches?

Although the question of ethical critique of the sacred scriptures has been raised with a new momentum since the 1990s, it is not, of course, a new question in either biblical or qur'anic hermeneutics.

Within a Protestant perspective, the need for an ethical critique might easily draw on the Lutheran principle of reading the Bible in light of its postulated centre, Christ. Although this hermeneutical principle was originally formulated by Luther to protect the *theological* message of salvation by faith alone against legalist interpretations, it has proved flexible and has also been used to define the *ethical* centre of the New Testament. The hermeneutical key would then be to establish a perceived centre *within* the message of Christ, as reflected not only in the Gospels but also in anti-legalistic parts of Paul's ethics. In the Church of Norway's recent discussions about homosexual partnership, this hermeneutical principle has been strongly activated (Kirkerådet 2006).

Similarly, in Islamic contexts, the old distinction between Meccan and Medinan suras has been activated by modern thinkers who have sought to reconcile the qur'anic message with human rights standards. For instance in Abullahi Ahmed an-Na'ims *Toward an Islamic Reformation. Civil Liberties, Human Rights, and International Law* (1990), he draws on his Sudanese teacher Mahmoud Mohamed Taha's reform methodology based on the concept of 'Islam's second message'. Similar to Christian liberal theology's distinction between Jesus and Paul, an-Na'im (inspired by Taha) suggests that the principle of abrogation (*naskh*) should be reversed so that the general admonitions of the Meccan suras should be given priority over against the detailed prescriptions of the Medinan ones:

> Muslims should shift the legal principle of Islamic law from one text [Medinan] of the Qur'an to the other [Meccan], from a text that was suitable to govern in the seventh century, and was implemented, to a text that was, at the time, too advanced and therefore had to be abrogated in effective legal terms. (an-Na'im 1990: 66f.)

An-Na'im also leans on Fazlur Rahman's distinction between basic values and concrete prescriptions in the Qur'an – another hermeneutical principle paralleled by similar distinctions in modern Christian hermeneutics aimed at reconciling the New Testament with modern moral sensibilities.

Why then have other scholars, both in Christianity and Islam, found it necessary to move beyond the cited hermeneutical approaches, towards a more direct, ethical dialogue with the scriptures? One reason is the recognition that the recognized moral problems cannot be confined to specific parts of the Scriptures. The problem is more comprehensive, and the foreignness of the Scriptures more fundamental. If so, the question of moral critique can only be tackled by taking more global, hermeneutical insights – for instance by leaning on readers' response theories.

Another reason why easy escapes must be abandoned is the insight that there will never be any global agreement on which ethical values should count as fundamental in the Scriptures. This is in fact also the problem with a so-called ethical critique of the Scriptures: who decides what should be counted as the basic moral problems (against which the Scriptures should be measured), and who defines the moral values by which the Scriptures should be enriched?

Transparency about who defines what as a moral problem is probably the only way ahead that might lead to an *enlightened* moral dialogue with the Scriptures, just as multiple interpretive spaces are the only way to avoid new forms of authoritarian interpretations (including liberal ones). Multiple interpretations correspond with the polysemic nature of scripture. As modern pluralism has blurred the borders between the religions and challenged established structures of authority, sacred scriptures, too, have revealed their polysemy and (from the perspective of Jacques Derrida) their – moral or religious – cracks.

Cracks may be seen as dangerous. But as Leonard Cohen has it, in his song 'Anthem': 'Forget your perfect offering. There is a crack in everything. That's how the light gets in.'

8

The Sacred Space between: A Relational Theology in Dialogue with Islam

The previous chapters have dealt with interreligious relations in philosophical, educational, ethical and political perspectives. What about theology?

During the last decades, the notion of 'theology of religion(s)' has been introduced as a reference to the self-reflection of a particular religious tradition when faced with religious pluralism. Alan Race used the expression 'Christian theology of religions' when in 1983 he introduced the oft-cited triad of exclusivism, inclusivism and pluralism (*Christians and Religious Pluralism*, 1983). Whereas Jaques Dupuis (1997) in his writings aimed at 'a Christian theology of religious pluralism', Harold Coward (2000) covered six religions when some years later he wrote about *Pluralism in the World Religions*. Paul Knitter moved from critically surveying 'Christian attitudes toward the world religions' (cf. the subtitle of *No Other Name*, 1985) to *Introducing Theologies of Religions* (2002, note the double plural).

Theologies of religions are created in response to religious pluralism. When reflecting theologically on the encounter between religions in modern pluralistic societies, we should keep in mind that there is a difference between traditional *plurality* and modern *pluralism*. Traditional plurality refers to a situation in which different cultures and faiths coexist as entities that can be neatly separated, in relatively stable constellations where religion is aligned with political power and the borders between the communities can only be crossed at great personal cost.

Whereas, in situations of traditional plurality, one particular tradition tends to be culturally and politically dominant, in situations of modern pluralism everything is more fluid. Dominant positions are challenged by modern ideals of equality and non-discrimination, and traditional stereotypes of the other are challenged by the development of multireligious societies and interreligious friendships.

At the personal level, individuals may identify with more than one culture and may develop plural identities. In the course of their lives, some individuals may also change their religious affiliation.

All major religions have their own ways of dealing with traditional plurality. But modern pluralism poses different kinds of challenges, which cut deeper and have potentially more wide-ranging consequences for the religious traditions. Modern pluralism also implies that every faith has to recognize a plurality of ethical and theological views within one's own tradition, a fact that further destabilizes conventional distinctions between ecumenical conversation and interreligious dialogue.

In what follows, I will reflect as a Christian theologian in dialogue with Islam. But how can these two traditions be neatly separated, intertwined as they are in history and contemporary societies? With regard to overarching theological reasoning, 'Christianity' (as an ecumenical whole) is certainly distinctively different from 'Islam'. But in the case of disagreement – be it ethical or theological – the fault lines do not coincide with the boundaries between the two religions.

Abandoning supersessionist claims?

Modern pluralism also destabilizes traditional perceptions (ecumenical as well as interreligious ones) of the supremacy of one's faith, reflecting the fact that all major religions and confessions have been conceived in situations of conflict. Many theologians claim that, in the context of modern pluralism, traditional ideas of supremacy and supersession must be abandoned just as – in political terms – hierarchical models for multireligious coexistence such as the Islamic *dhimmi* system must be replaced with equal citizenship.

In an article from 2007, titled 'My God is bigger that your God'. Time for another axial shift in the history of religion', Paul Knitter notes that theology is not just about God – it has also to do with earthly claims of superiority:

> Religious people who make universal claims of superiority believe that it is God's will that, if not now than eventually, all people will become or should become members of their divinely constituted superior religion . . . We come to what is for me the most impelling reason why the religions are being called to an axial shift regarding claims of superiority: the link between claims of religious superiority and privilege and calls to religious aggression and violence. (Knitter 2007: 103, 105)

Critically aware of the potentially violent consequences of traditional claims of supremacy, Knitter calls for a shift from superior truth claims to what he calls 'the mutuality model', in which 'many true religions [are] called to dialogue' (Knitter 2002: 109ff.). He strongly believes that such an 'axial shift' is in fact possible, because of what he calls the mystical and the ethical-prophetic elements in all religions which – in his terminology – constitute 'bridges' between religious traditions that may otherwise seem to be worlds apart.

Catherine Cornille, in her book *The Im-Possibility of Interreligious Dialogue* (2008) expresses a similar view when under the heading of 'Interconnection' she speaks of ethical issues as 'common external challenges' and mystical traditions as 'common experience'. It is not clear, however, why Cornille sees ethical concerns such as sustainable development and alleviation of suffering as 'external' challenges. In Knitter's reasoning, the ethical bridge seems, rather, to be conceived of as an 'internal' construction built on the religions' strong prophetic traditions.

Knitter's solution to the seemingly unsurpassable problem of superlative language in the religious traditions, such as the proclamation of Jesus as the only way, is to see such expressions as a kind of 'love language' meant for internal consumption only. He also calls for a dialogical Christology which – in conjunction with John Cobb – sees Christ as 'the Way which is open to Other Ways' (Knitter 2002: 119–23, 156f.).

Such solutions to modern annoyances with claims of supremacy seem not, however, to be acceptable to other theologians who would otherwise be ready to tread the ethical and mystical bridges between the religions. For instance, in an article from 1999 titled 'The Last Trump Card: Islam and the Supersession of Other Faiths', the Islamic theologian Tim Winter (*aka* Abdul-Hakim Murad) criticizes Paul Knitter, John Hick and Muslim pluralist theologians such as Fazlur Rahman, Farid Esack and Mahmoud Ayoub for identifying supersessionist claims with confrontation:

> Hick, Knitter and their Muslim travelling-companions are . . . mistaken in suggesting that foundational claims for the present centrality of one's own community in salvation history ineluctably lead believers towards *hubris*, discord and confrontation. (Winter 1999: 152)

According to Winter, the doctrine of Islam's abrogation (*naskh*) of prior religions is constitutive of Islam itself: 'As in its treatment of Judaism, but more sharply, the Muslim revelation deploys arguments against a historically-evolved Christianity in order to justify the latest divine intervention' (Winter 1999: 142). However, Winter does not see Islamic supersessionist claims as a problem in itself for dialogue in modern pluralistic societies: 'Supersessionism . . . has negative implications for dialogue only when read as cause for triumphalism, rather than as a spur to the contrite awareness of a heavy responsibility' (1999: 152).

In Winter's view, 'The surest sign of a supersessionism that is humble, and seeks the esteem rather than the alienation of earlier communities, is a commitment to the struggle against oppression and injustice' (1999: 153). With the latter formulation, Winter seems to join Paul Knitter and Farid Esack (cf. Esack's book: *Qur'an, Liberation and Pluralism. An Islamic Perspective of Interreligious Solidarity Against Oppression*, 1997) in the conviction that joint struggle against oppression and injustice may constitute a firm bridge between people of different religious affiliations. However, as he has also demonstrated in a polemical review of Esack's book (Murad n.d.), Tim Winter sees no need to reconsider theological claims of supersession in light of modern experiences of interreligious cooperation.

Against Winter, it is hard to see how supersessionist claims can *not* be associated with political claims of supremacy or – at least – heavily coloured by established majority/minority constellations. It should be remembered, however, that theological claims of supersession are not always wedded to political power. In minority situations, supremacy claims may function instead as a kind of political protest, quite similar to the way in which both the Jesus movement and Muhammad's prophetic mission initially took shape in opposition to established power structures. But contemporary theological reflection cannot overlook the fact that both religions have historically functioned as religions of power, and that claims of supremacy have generally come to be associated with political majority positions – or ambitions to achieve such power.

Towards a relational theology in dialogue with Islam

In Chapter 2, I tried to demonstrate how the writings of Martin Buber and Emmanuel Levinas have elucidated my own reflection on the philosophy of dialogue. In what follows, I will try out a theological reasoning that (in Buber's sense) is *relational* and (in Levinas' sense) marked by a concern for human vulnerability and the *humanization of theology*.

In my outline of a relational theology, I will structure my discussion according to a Trinitarian scheme of reasoning. How can essential elements of the Christian belief in the Creator, in Jesus Christ and in the Holy Spirit give sense in a dialogue with Islam? Trying to avoid the imposition of Christian theological models on the conversation, I will formulate my Trinitarian reflections as a response to challenges posed by the Qur'an, a Shi'ite theologian – and a Jewish thinker.

Christian theologians conventionally characterize Trinitarian theology as a relational understanding of divine reality. Trinitarian theology is regularly associated with the mystery of love, reflecting a recognition that the belief that 'God is love' can only be expressed in relational terms – for instance in the image of mutual love between father and son, or in an understanding of holy spirit as the power of love that holds everything together. Thus in his response to the Muslim dialogue initiative *A Common Word* (referred to in Chapter 3), Archbishop Rowan Williams writes:

> Because God exists in this threefold pattern of interdependent action, the relationship between Father, Son and Holy Spirit is one in which there is always a 'giving place' to each other, each standing back so that the other may act. The only human language we have for this is love. (Williams 2008)

The question is how a theological understanding of the relational nature of love can be translated from a meditation on the nature of the divine to a reflection on how theology can be shaped in living relationships with – or in the sacred space between – believers of different faiths.

Is religious plurality willed by the Creator?

A fundamental challenge posed by the Qur'an to Christians in all times and places is to see religious plurality as something willed by God. As regards the first article of faith, in the Creator, dialogically minded Muslims are still waiting for a Christian response to what they perceive as the Qur'an's acceptance of religious plurality as divinely instituted. Some well-known and oft-cited verses of the fifth sura read as follows:

> It was We who revealed the Law (to Moses): therein was guidance and light . . . Let the people of the Gospel judge by what Allah hath revealed therein . . . To each among you have we prescribed a law (*shir'a*) and an open way (*minhaj*). If Allah had so willed, He would have made you a single people (*umma*), but His plan is to test you in what He hath given you: so strive as in a race in all virtues. The goal of you all is to Allah; it is He that will show you the truth of the matters in which ye dispute. (Sura 5: 44, 47f. – in Yusuf Ali's translation)[1]

In this passage, the historical fact of religious plurality is seen as a divinely willed test for humanity, in which each people (or community) is seeking to implement the will of God in accordance with the revelation they have received and the path (*shir'a*, a cognate of *shari'a*) to which they have been guided. Sura 49: 13 seems also to associate cultural – and possibly, religious – diversity with something willed by God: 'O mankind! We created you from a single (pair) of a male and a female, and made you into nations and tribes, that ye may know each other not that ye may despise (each other).'

There are, however, other passages in the Qur'an that point in a different direction. For instance in sura 2 – which for a large part is dedicated to the demarcation between Islam and the People of the Book – differences in religious matters are seen as a result of human selfishness (sura 2: 213). In the most polemical passages, Christians and Jews are chastised as *kafirun* because they are perceived as having 'covered up' some central aspects of God's will.[2]

On may also ask how inclusive the quoted passage from sura 5 actually is, in light of a different verse in the same literary context: 'Oh ye who believe! Take not the Jews and the Christians for your friends and protectors!' (5: 51) Although the latter verse might seem to circumscribe any 'pluralist' implication of the preceding verses, it could also be read as a warning not to blur the distinctions between the three different Abrahamic faiths – as it is precisely the differences ('to each of you we have prescribed a law') that are meant to serve as a divinely constituted fundament for the competition in good works.

The quoted passages from sura 5 have been subject to quite contrary interpretations by Muslim theologians, ranging from conservative exclusivism to modernist inclusivist or pluralist interpretations (Esack 1997: 166ff.; Sirry 2009). But the question remains of how Christians will respond to the fundamental qur'anic acceptance of religious plurality as a divine *test* and a potential *blessing*.

This has also to do with how we see the other's scriptures. When the Muslim signatories of *A Common Word* quote the Qur'an and the Bible side by side, they implicitly dissociate themselves from cruder versions of the *tahrif* dogma,[3] treating instead central aspects of the Bible as reliable revelation. How do Christians respond to that, with regard to the Qur'an? In the Archbishop of Canterbury's response to *A Common Word* (Williams 2008), which is very rich in biblical references, he also quotes verses from the Qur'an. Implicitly, he treats the holy book of Islam as a divine source of spiritual guidance.

Are Christians ready to pursue this course? The movement known as 'scriptural reasoning' (Ford and Pecknold 2006), in which Christians, Jews and Muslims meditate and reflect together on texts from the Bible, the Qur'an and Hadith, seems to imply a deep acceptance of the Others' scriptures. In such practices, a double experience is often made: a sense of joint blessing, but also a recognition that differences in scriptural interpretation do not necessarily coincide with the boundaries between religions. Although the theological consequences of such experiences remain to be spelled out, it seems that practices of scriptural reasoning have the potential of engendering a kind of theology that is as relational as the reading experiences underlying it.

In a Trinitarian scheme, the question at stake is whether and how human experiences of deep sharing across religious differences can be interpreted as a sign of divinely created diversity; that is, as part of the belief in the Creator.

Can Christ be a common sign?

For me, the double experience of joint blessings and challenging differences in interreligious encounters resonates with an article that was written by

Hasan Askari (an Indian-British Muslim of Shiʿite background) as early as in 1972, entitled 'The dialogical relationship between Christianity and Islam' (Askari 1972; cf. Leirvik 2010a: 258f.). The double context of Askari's writings is his experience from multireligious societies in India and Britain, and his commitment to Muslim-Christian dialogue on the international scene.

In dialogue, existence for Askari means inter-existence: 'Each man becomes a neighbour' (Askari 1972: 481). In this inter-existence,[4] neither the living neighbour nor the divine truth can be objectified. Reminiscent of Martin Buber, Askari seems to associate objectification with monological communication. In his reflection on the dialogical relation, Askari warns against the monological tendency in both religions, suggesting that 'the monological trap' can only be escaped if Christians and Muslims engage each other in an open conversation about how to understand the signs of God:

> The truth is that Christianity and Islam constitute one complex of faith, one starting with the Person, and another with the Word. Their separateness does not denote two areas of conflicting truths, but a dialogical necessity. (Askari 1972: 485)

According to Askari, reading the revealed signs of God in a dialogical way is different from both objectifying the Word of God in a Book (the potential Muslim fallacy) and identifying it with a particular Person (the corresponding Christian one). Convinced that Christianity and Islam constitute 'a dialogical whole', Askari speaks of Christ as a common sign of God for Christians and Muslims. Plunging deep into the mystery of dialogue, Askari states that 'Unity is had when a religious sign is shared.' Since Christ is a common sign for Christians and Muslims, Askari suggests that 'Once having known Christ is to belong together' (Askari 1972: 485).

When Askari speaks of Christ as a common sign and divine revelation as essentially dialogical, this has nothing to do with harmonizing away religious differences. Recognizing that Christ is regarded as a divine sign in both religions, but interpreted in painfully different ways, Askari suggests that it belongs to the very nature of a divine sign that it is interpreted in different ways. The fact of conflicting interpretations should not be regarded as a threat but, rather, as a reflection of what a divine sign implies:

> A common religious sign must be differently apprehended. It is the very ambiguity, richness, of the religious sign that gives rise to different and even

> opposed interpretations and understandings [in this case, of Christ]. (Askari 1972: 485)

On the human level, pain is related to the discovery of the other's irreducible difference: 'To drop monologue is to immediately discover the other.' However,

> [t]he discovery of the other, of our own being, is both soothing and painful, more the latter. The other is pain, a sting, a bite, but a pain in our very being, of it. It is right in the middle of this pain and anxiety that a Divine Sign is known. (Askari 1972: 486)

The Christian theologian Michael Barnes makes it a general point in the understanding of human communication when (with references to Levinas) he notes that 'In whatever I do and say, I am faced by other persons who put my self-sufficiency into question' (Barnes 2002: 72). Askari seems to imply that Christian-Muslim conversation is even more challenging, but also uniquely rewarding. If Christians and Muslims venture a joint reading of the signs of God, in a friendship that is potentially painful, they might experience even a deeper, but shared suffering:

> Thrown in front of God, facing this deep, vast Absolute, Christians and Muslims will undergo the second pain, far acuter, wider and sharper than the first. This is Second Suffering. It is here that God meets man, and man meets Christ. It was in this state that Mohammed heard the Word of God. (Askari 1972: 486)

This is Askari's way of reasoning about religious plurality before God: the Creator has left signs for the human being that can be interpreted differently. Can Christians follow Askari in this line of reasoning? Or do they feel that such an open approach to divine signs compromises their Christian faith in Christ?

In my own reflections on Christology in dialogue with Islam (Leirvik 2010a), I have suggested that serious theological conversation with Islam may lead to a rethinking of classical formulations of the mystery of incarnation, divine sonship and the meaning of the cross. The point is not to take away what is different from Islamic convictions in Christian beliefs about Christ. That would go against Askari's reminder that the divine mystery can only be approached in respect of real differences in how Christ is understood in the two religions.

Nevertheless, there are some unnecessary stumbling blocks that may be removed – in order to facilitate an open conversation about the sign of Christ. For instance, Olaf Schumann in his (1988) book *Der Christus der Muslime* ('The Christ of the Muslims') critically examines notions of divine sonship that have been wedded not only to Christian claims of supremacy but also to political power. He advocates instead a Servant Christology that is sensitive to Muslim sensibilities and still true to basic Christian teachings. Admitting that notions like 'Son of God' and 'Lord' had become part of a power language long before the Islamic era,[5] Schumann suggests that the Qur'an might thus have been 'contextually right' in rejecting the notion 'Son of God'. Instead, the Qur'an venerates Jesus as Servant of God.

In his Christian response, Schumann recalls the fact that according to the (synoptic) Gospels, Jesus himself was reluctant to accept the title 'Son of God'. Instead, he refers to himself as 'Son of Man', and acts as a Servant, not as a Lord. In the early Christian hymn preserved in the Letter to the Philippians 2.5–11, Jesus is portrayed as the obedient Servant/Slave of God, who, despite his origins in God, chose to be in human likeness, assuming the nature of a servant/slave, humbling himself to the point of death on the cross.

Speaking from within Christian sensibilities, Schumann raises the question of whether the cross can be acceptable to Muslims as the deepest expression of Jesus' humanity and his obedience to God; that is not as a failure, but as faithfulness: 'Christ's humility in his service and his obedience to the will of his Father did not stop *before* the cross, but included it.' And maybe even more important for a Muslim awareness: 'Only on the cross, through the final submission of will and its ambition "to be like God" may the always present temptation of "*širk*" be defeated' (Schumann 1988: 178).[6]

Referring to the more mundane conceptions of divine power in Islam, Schumann concludes his reflections by asking the Muslims whether a political understanding of God's rule is really defensible in theological terms. From the Christian side,

> Jesus' refusal to identify the Kingdom of God with a political understanding of society or state . . . is not seen as a deficiency. On the contrary, the confusion of God's kingdom with society and state is seen as an unholy temptation. (Schumann 1988: 179)[7]

Would it be thinkable, although by now mostly un-thought, that Christians and Muslims together might overcome the temptations of absolute power, in critical awareness of human vulnerability and in a shared confession that ultimate meaning and power rest only with God?

As can be seen with Schumann, rethinking Christian Christology might be good for more than preaching Christ in more sensitive ways in an Islamic context. It touches upon questions of general relevance in interreligious dialogue.

Relational Pneumatology

Before pursuing my Christological reflections on power, suffering and vulnerability by approaching the issue of a humanization of theology, I will briefly touch upon the question of a relational Pneumatology. What I have in mind is Martin Buber's philosophy of dialogue which was introduced in Chapter 2 and includes a relational way of understanding the work of the Holy Spirit. The main ethical point in Buber's philosophy of dialogue is to avoid reducing one another to an object, an 'It'. Like Askari, he associates objectification with monologue (2002: 22f.).

If, instead, in a dialogical relation, we treat each other as I and Thou, something sacred takes place in the space between. In an essay on dialogue, Buber speaks of it as 'communion' (2002: 6). He even characterizes true dialogue as a sacrament, 'where unreserve has ruled, even wordlessly, between men, the word of dialogue has happened sacramentally' (2002: 5; cf. 21).

If in a truly dialogical relation, we treat each other as I and Thou, the space between us will be filled by Spirit. When in *I and Thou* Buber speaks of the realm of between, he explicitly refers to it as the place of the Spirit: 'Spirit is not in the I, but between I and Thou . . . Man lives in the spirit, if he is able to respond to his Thou . . . Only in virtue of his power to enter into relation is he able to live in the spirit' (Buber 1987: 57f.).

In later writings, Buber elaborates his relational philosophy and speaks of the 'sphere' or the 'realm' of between. As noted in Chapter 2, the *realm of between* is the sphere in which true dialogue takes place, as a third dimension beyond the individual and social aspects of existence: 'On the far side of the subjective, on this side of the objective, on the narrow ridge, where I and Thou meet, there is the realm of "between"' (Buber 2002: 243).

Buber's horizon of dialogue was mainly a Jewish-Christian one. Does this kind of relational theology, or Pneumatology, give sense in Christian-Muslim dialogue? I believe it does, because this way of reasoning protects the sanctity of every true encounter, whether it is experienced as a blessing or as a difficult test. It reveals both modes of interreligious encounter as a potential dwelling place of the Holy Spirit.

Towards a humanization of theological ethics?

With its focus on interpersonal relations, my theological reflections in dialogue with Islam can be read as an expression of an ethical turn in theology (cf. Chapter 7). Whereas theologies of religion are often self-centred, in the sense of being focused on how to understand one's own faith in relation to what others believe, ethics (at least in Levinas' sense) is fundamentally oriented towards the human Other.

What, then, would an ethical, other-directed theology of religions look like? Is it possible – interreligiously – to formulate a theology of religion that is fundamentally relational, oriented towards the vulnerable other, and open for a humanization of theological ethics?

In terms of systematic theology, Olaf Schumann's Christological reflections on sonship and servanthood, with its critical perspective on power language and its orientation towards vulnerability, can in fact be read as a humanization of Christology. In late modern philosophies of religion, we have seen (in Chapter 2) that the Jewish philosopher Emmanuel Levinas regards the face of the Other as an epiphany of God: 'The wonderful thing about the face is that is *speaks*, it says: need, vulnerability, it asks, begs *me* of help, it makes me responsible . . . God, the god, it's long way there, a road that goes via the Other. Loving God is Loving the Other' (1993: 214f.).[8] Correspondingly, Michael Barnes in his Christian version of a Levinas-inspired theology of dialogue speaks of 'discovering the face of Christ' when facing the religious Other (2002: 238ff.).

The frame of reference for Levinas and Schumann is of course the Jewish-Christian tradition, in which the human Other is often seen as an epiphany of God, literally standing between the Self and God. For instance, in Genesis

33.10, when Jacob returns from his exile to meet his brother Esau whom he had once cunningly cheated, Jacob presents his gift of reconciliation with the following words: 'If I have found favour in your eyes, accept this gift from me. For to see your face is like seeing the face of God, now that you have received me favourably.' In the New Testament, 1 John 4.20 proclaims that 'anyone who does not love his brother, whom he has seen, cannot love God, whom he has not seen.' And in the judgement scene of Matthew 25, Jesus is foreseen to say on the Day of Judgement, with reference to the treatment of the hungry, the thirsty, the naked, the sick, the imprisoned and the strangers: 'Truly I tell you, whatever you did [not] for one of the least of these brothers and sisters of mine, you did [not] for me.'

As mentioned, the Muslim dialogue initiative *A Common Word* suggests that the uniting bond between Muslims and Christians should be the double commandment of love, in which love of God can never be separated from 'loving your brother as yourself'.[9] Differently from the picture of Muslim theology given in *A Common Word*, Islam is generally seen as a religion in which the distance between God and the human being is too vast to be bridged by human love. There are, however, other strands in Islamic theology in which the notion of love unites the human and the divine. Islamic mysticism has a long, poetic tradition of obliterating the distinction between human and divine love, as when Rumi proclaims:

> For lovers, the only teaching is the beauty of the Beloved:
> their only book and lecture is the Face.
> Outwardly they are silent,
> but their penetrating remembrance rises
> to the high throne of their Friend.
> Their only lesson is enthusiasm, whirling, and trembling,
> not the minor details of law.[10]

With regard to ethical reasoning, qur'anic ethics seems ultimately aimed at attaining proximity to God. The Qur'an may even speak of the desire for 'God's face' (*wajh Allah*) as the ultimate aim of a righteous life (sura 2: 272; 6: 52). And with regard to the Jewish-Christian idea of the vulnerable Other standing between myself and God, a famous hadith about the merit of visiting the sick in the collection of Sahih Muslim comes astonishingly close to the judgement scene in Matthew 25:

> Abu Huraira reported Allah's Messenger (may peace be upon him) as saying: Verily, Allah, the Exalted and Glorious, would say on the Day of Resurrection: O son of Adam, I was sick but you did not visit Me. He would say: O my Lord; how could I visit Thee whereas Thou art the Lord of the worlds? Thereupon He would say: Didn't you know that such and such servant of Mine was sick but you did not visit him and were you not aware of this that if you had visited him, you would have found Me by him (*la-wajadtani 'indahu*)? O son of Adam, I asked food from you but you did not feed Me. He would say: My Lord, how could I feed Thee whereas Thou art the Lord of the worlds? He said: Didn't you know that such and such servant of Mine asked food from you but you did not feed him, and were you not aware that if you had fed him you would have found him by My side (*dhalik 'indi*)? (The Lord would again say:) O son of Adam, I asked drink from you but you did not provide Me. He would say: My Lord, how could I provide Thee whereas Thou art the Lord of the worlds? Thereupon He would say: Such and such of servant of Mine asked you for a drink but you did not provide him, and had you provided him drink you would have found him near Me (*dhalik 'indi*).[11]

Interestingly, other translations render the expression *dhalik 'indi* ('found him by My side', 'found him near Me') as 'retrieved it by Me'[12] – referring probably to a heavenly reward or loss ('it') instead of a vulnerable human ('him') behind whom God is found. But the other reading, in which God intimately identifies himself with the suffering human being, seems to be just as plausible.

Whether or not the above hadith should be taken as a loan from the New Testament or not, it testifies to the fact the idea of God standing by the side of the vulnerable human being is in fact a shared motif between Christianity and Islam. When *A Common Word* links love of God and love of the other as intimately as it does, I take this as a possible point of departure for a dialogue on humanization of theology and ethics.

The important question is of course what concrete consequences a humanization of theological ethics might have. In March 2005, Tariq Ramadan called for an immediate moratorium on the death penalty and *hudud* punishments (such as corporeal punishment for theft and for illegitimate sexual relationships) in the Muslim world.[13] The intention behind the call, Ramadan explains, was to address

> the conscience of each individual, to mobilise ordinary Muslims to call on their governments to place an immediate moratorium on the application of these punishments, and to call for Muslim scholars for the opening of a vast intra-community debate on the matter. (Ramadan 2009: 165)

When reading his call, it struck me that the guiding principle behind his moratorium was clearly a theologically motivated concern for the vulnerable human being. Ramadan realizes that, in an imperfect world with asymmetrical power relations, severe punishments will regularly hit women more than men and the poorer and weaker members of society more frequently than the wealthy and powerful ones. If we recognize this sombre reality, says Ramadan, 'it is impossible for us as Muslims to remain silent as irreversible injustice is done to the poorest and weakest members of society in the name of our religion' (2009: 163).

Muslim reactions against the proposed moratorium proved its controversial character, whereas some Western reactions implied that Ramadan should have called for a full abolition of *hudud* punishments and not merely a 'moratorium'. The way Ramadan argues his proposed moratorium, however, gives the impression that his call is really meant for an indefinite period of time, probably for ever. For, from Ramadan's perspective, how can such punishments ever be justified, as long as human injustice exists?

Ethical concern for the vulnerable human being is clearly the implied premise for Ramadan's moratorium. I therefore take his call as a recent example of humanizing theological reasoning in Islam. In Ramadan's case, his application of the humane criterion in theological reasoning leads him to sidestep important aspects of classical Sharia – for the sake of humanity.

A similar line of reasoning was expressed by Arwa al-Tawil, a female member of the Muslim Brotherhood who took an active part in the Tahrir demonstrations in 2011, when commenting upon violent demonstrations in Afghanistan against the burning of the Qur'an by two American pastors: 'Life is more sacred than the Qur'an . . . A mad pastor burning a Qur'an does not justify killings. A life is more holy than the Qur'an in Islam.'[14]

Religious and secular concerns

In preceding chapters, I have demonstrated how long-term Christian-Muslim dialogue, focused on vulnerability, has opened up for a fundamental reassessment of classical positions, for instance as regards the rights of religious minorities, the individual's right to change his or her religious belonging, gender justice and the issue of homosexuality. The (Lutheran) Church of Norway has increasingly come to see these issues as interrelated, since they all touch upon the integrity of vulnerable groups and individuals.

From the cited themes, one might perhaps think that the churches in Norway are pressing a liberal agenda in some of these issues. I would rather say that the issues in question arise from the context, and from a shared public culture in Scandinavia. Imbued with egalitarian and feminist thought, public discourses in the Norwegian context constantly challenge Christians and Muslims alike to reconsider their traditional positions – and to 'humanize' their theologies.

This means also to make them more gender-just. As indicated by the following statement from a former leader of the Muslim Students' Association, Bushra Ishaq (when commenting on increased subscription to values of gender equality), processes of change in Muslim gender relations cannot be grasped unless in a contextual perspective: 'Were it not for the fundamental influence of Norwegian culture and the values of the welfare state, the emerging Muslim feminism would not be a matter of fact.'[15]

In humanizing theological ethics, then, Christians and Muslims are not merely in dialogue with each other but with secular society as well (cf. my reasoning about interreligious dialogue and secularity in Chapter 3).

9

Interreligious Studies and Interfaith Dialogue, in Academia

In Chapter 1, I introduced the notion of interreligious studies as a relational approach to religious activism and the study of religion. Following the discussion of interreligious studies as an academic discipline, the question arises: How should one understand interreligious *studies* in relation to dialogical *practice* and interfaith *education*?

In academia, 'interreligious studies' may refer to education and research carried out by researchers who have different backgrounds in terms of religion and life stances. However, when for instance Christian and Muslim researchers work together in departments of religious studies or in multireligious faculties of theology, their scholarly communication may also take the form of reflective dialogue. The same is true for learning processes between students of different faith backgrounds.

Thus the distinction between interreligious studies and interfaith dialogue is hard to make in practice, and also in the academic context. It would be simplistic to see interfaith dialogue solely as an object of study. Insights from dialogue may also affect the way in which religion is studied and taught in the academy.

As interreligious studies is a relatively new academic discipline, there is still a lack of scholarly contributions which may elucidate the field theoretically. In the following, I will note Ursula King, Jeannine Hill Fletcher and Anne Hege Grung's gender theoretical perspective on interreligious studies before I discuss Scott Daniel Dunbar and David Cheetham's rather different perspectives on interfaith dialogue and interreligious studies in the academic context. I will also relate my reflections to Gavin Flood's (1999) book *Beyond Phenomenology*.

Critical gender perspectives

In an article from 1998, Ursula King discusses feminism as a missing dimension of interreligious dialogue. She notes that institutionalized dialogues more often than not lack both female participants and a critical gender perspective that might shed light on gendered power imbalances in the faith communities.

In King's perspective, gender critique sheds light not only on the social phenomenon of interreligious dialogue but simultaneously on the academic study of religion:

> It is characteristic of religious feminism that it is not only an academic method which envisages *how* religions are *studied*, but it also embraces a new and religious vision which affects *what* religion is, i.e. *how* religions are *lived and practiced* . . . this critical, feminist dialogue of women challenges or potentially even subverts interreligious dialogue as it is conducted at present. (King 1998: 42, 47)

Jeannine Hill Fletcher (2013) has taken King's critical gender reflections a step further by discussing the issue of 'Women in Inter-Religious Dialogue' in relation to three different models of dialogue: the 'parliament' model, the 'activist' model and the 'storytelling' model. Whereas the representative parliament model – by leaning on institutional leadership – has tended to marginalize women, the activist and storytelling models are more open to women's agency. They are also more oriented towards transformation – not only of the religions but of the category of religion itself:

> If the Parliament Model carves out distinctive things that are 'the religions' and separates them out for comparison, it also falls prey to a pattern of privileging 'religion' over and against other realities. The Activist Model sees religion intimately intertwined with other realities of our human existence, and calls religion to task for the way it can be coopted within these realities to undermine human wellbeing. (Fletcher 2013: 177)

Similar points have been made by Anne Hege Grung in her feminist analyses of interreligious dialogue. She suggests that including a critical gender perspective would not only mean addressing particular themes concerning women in the religious communities. It also means to apply a gender-sensitive openness and a gender perspective when discussing *all* themes and issues in the dialogues (Grung 2011a: 73; cf. Grung 2008: 297). The same would of course apply to critical gender *studies* of dialogue practices.

Education for or studies of dialogue?

Contributions that more directly address the question of interreligious studies or interfaith dialogue in the academic context reflect the more general question of theology and religious studies. In an article from 1998, titled 'The place of interreligious dialogue in the academic study of religion', Scott Daniel Dunbar also raises the fundamental question of 'whether the practice of interreligious dialogue is compatible with the academic study of religion'. In his understanding, this is just a variant of the larger question of the relationship between theology and religion studies in the academia:

> The academic study of religion was intended to be nonsectarian and impartial as an alternative to theological studies; in contrast, interreligious dialogue presupposes religious commitments because it involves at least two persons from different religions conversing together about issues of religious significance. (Dunbar 1998: 455)

Dunbar seems thus to regard interfaith dialogue as a mode of theology, because dialogue requires both a religious commitment and a recognition of religious agency. Conversely, religious studies are likely to be critical of any attempt to introduce something like interfaith dialogue in the academic context. Unfolding his reasoning, Dunbar, not surprisingly, attacks the 'myth of objectivity' which he believes still influences religious studies and informs religion scholars' scepticism towards interreligious dialogue.

Dunbar does not use the concept of interreligious studies. His mission is to advocate the academic respectability of interreligious dialogue. He does so by supplementing religious studies' purely *descriptive* study of religion with what he calls *prescriptive* and *experience-oriented* ('experiential') studies of religion:

> Descriptive study is useful because it records and documents the dialogue process for the present and future generations. Prescriptive study introduces

> students to more thought-provoking questions, such as: Can interreligious dialogue play a role in resolving religious conflicts and healing past injustices? Can insights on 'truth' arise in dialogue? Can interreligious dialogue help liberate groups from religious oppression? Finally, experiential study helps students study to understand the dynamics of interreligious dialogue in a more existential way that has practical implications for their own lives. Thus, all the above approaches to dialogue have a place in the academic study of religion. (Dunbar 1998: 462)

Dunbar's approach to interfaith dialogue as an academic activity is clearly a theological – even practical theological – one. Correspondingly, he would probably have great trouble trying to convince religious studies that interfaith dialogue is not just an object of critical studies but can also be seen as a value-based activity that the university – in tune with its social responsibility – should promote, with corresponding admonitions to the students to get involved in interreligious dialogue.

A more distanced approach to 'interfaith education' in the university context can be found in an article by David Cheetham from 2005. In accordance with his academic base at the University of Birmingham, Cheetham represents the characteristic synthesis of 'theology and religious studies' which can be found in many British universities. The University of Birmingham has for a long time been at the forefront of the study of Christian-Muslim relations and interreligious relations in general.

Cheetham starts out with a reflection on the name of a new master's programme that the University of Birmingham introduced at the beginning of the twenty-first century. When the idea of a new programme arose, it was with the label of 'interfaith dialogue'. But when the programme was launched, the name changed to 'inter-religious relations'. In this way, says Cheetham, it tried to meet the aspirations of both the dialogue enthusiasts and the more critical or reluctant ones, as well as the demands from students who had more general academic interests in interfaith relations. Although Cheetham, like Dunbar, argues that the university should play a role in 'interfaith education', he more clearly distinguishes between the *descriptive* study of interfaith relations on the one hand and *prescriptive* forms of interreligious education with a goal 'to educate people towards a culture of dialogue and mutual exchange' on the other.

Can the university make space for both of these approaches to interreligious encounters? In Cheetham's view, this should be possible but only if the secular university abandons its modern objectivity paradigm and opens up for a more pluralistic and postmodern way of thinking about the relationship between religion and secularity.

For Cheetham, interreligious studies also has to do with the academic legitimacy of theology. In the British context, theology's place in the secular university had already been subject to a protracted – and for theology's part, defensive – debate. Cheetham notes, however, that from the late 1990s some theologians (especially Gavin d'Costa and Gavin Hyman) have taken a more offensive approach. Acknowledging that value of neutrality in religious studies is unrealistic and perhaps not desirable, theologians have challenged 'religious studies' to explain their values (d'Costa 1998).

Cheetham argues that the study of interreligious relations has its legitimate place as a university study, but is also critical of too much emphasis on what Dunbar calls 'Prescriptive study': 'it is difficult to see how the study of interreligious relations could be *prescribed* in such a way that the typical outcomes are "respect", "tolerance" or "a culture of peace and dialogue"' (Cheetham 2005: 30).

Cheetham concludes that the study of interreligious relations (including the critical study of the phenomenon of religious dialogue) may actually profit from being anchored in a secular university. This anchoring, he suggests, may give study programmes in interreligious relations a necessary distance from pious ambitions of contributing to peace and tolerance, and allow for more diverse and also more conflict-oriented approaches.

According to Cheetham, it is precisely the *complexity* of the multireligious landscape that should be the focus of interreligious studies. The educational challenge would then be to find the best ways to make students 'properly literate with regard to the concerns of different religion, the problem of conflicting truth-claims, historical factors and issues concerning the future of interreligious encounter' (2005: 33).

Living and researching the space in between

As explained in Chapter 2, in my own contributions to the philosophy of dialogue and the theory of interreligious studies, inspired by Martin Buber I have been using the metaphor of 'the space in between'. Whereas Dunbar and Cheetham have primarily discussed what should be the horizon of interreligious education courses, I have also tried to reflect on the role of the researcher in the study of what takes place in the dynamic encounter between religions (and their living representatives).

In a broad, sociological perspective, it is difficult to see how anyone – quite independently of whether one is religiously active or not – should be able to posit oneself outside of the cultural and religious encounters and explore them from a completely detached position. Such insights render the old distinction between a (theological) insider perspective and a (religious studies) outsider perspective not so meaningful:

> In interreligious studies, i.e. studies of the relationship between religions, the research task is even more complex: What does it means to be 'inside' or 'outside' the shared space between religions and life stances? Does not everyone have a part in the space between? (Leirvik 2006c: 117)

This means that anyone who ventures a description of the relationship between the religions, and between religious and secular world views, must be able to explain where he or she places themselves in the landscape.

My reflections at this point tune in with Gavin Flood's remarks on 'Dialogue and the situated observer', in his book *Beyond Phenomenology* (1999). Referring to the shift to language and the sign as the focus of religious and cultural studies, Flood criticizes the idea of 'the detached, epistemic subject penetrating the alien world of the other through the phenomenological process'. Instead, Flood writes, 'the subject must be defined in relation to other subjects'. Religious studies thus become

> a dialogical enterprise in which the inquirer is situated within a particular context or narrative tradition, and whose research into narrative traditions, that become the objects of investigation, must be apprehended in a much richer and multi-faceted way. . . . The relationship between the situated observer and situation of observation, becomes dialogical in the sense that the observer is thrown into conversation with people and texts of the object tradition. (1999: 143)

'Rather than the disengaged reason of the social scientists observing, recording and theorizing data', Flood suggests, 'we have a situation in which research is imaged as "conversation", or more accurately "critical conversation", in which the interactive nature of research is recognized.'

Flood's main theoretical reference at this point is the philosopher and literary critic Mikhail Bakhtin, who understands research as 'inquiry and observations, that is, dialogue' (1999: 143). In light of the Norwegian sociologist Hans Skjervheim's (1996) reflections on spectator- and participant positions one might argue that neither the observer nor the space between which is observed are stable facts that can be objectively ascertained. The critical reflection on how to place oneself in unstable and contestable spaces also makes it impossible to assume that taking a neutral 'middle position' should in any way be possible. The research-ethical requirement must, rather, be transparency as regards the individual's own position. In this way, research on the space in between is left open to discussion. In that way, a kind of objectivity that is not resting on the individual but on critical intersubjectivity, can be achieved (Leirvik 2006c: 118).

Philosophically and theologically, the realm of between may be spoken of as the realm of the Spirit. Sociologically and politically, the space in between is contested space, in which religions and world views must find ways to coexist. In terms or research, the space in between can only be properly investigated when the researcher recognizes his or her role as a participating agent in what takes place in shared spaces.

The space in between can also be seen as the space of ethical inquiry and critique. Both practitioners and researchers may confront – or critically analyse – cultural practices and religious traditions in the light of ethically charged convictions which in the modern context are often shared across religious divides. In this sense, both Buber's realm of between and Bhabha's third space (cf. Chapter 3) can be thought of as the space of ethics.

Postscript: United against Extremism?

'Extremism' is a difficult word fraught with shifting political connotations. As a political or religious notion, extremism seems to presuppose an idea of normality – which can then be envisaged as a middle point between extremist deviations to the 'right' or the 'left' (hence the distinction between right-wing- and left-wing-extremism).

In practice, however, there is no general agreement of what should be counted as more or less severe 'deviations' from the perceived norm or centre. For instance, in an interreligious declaration from a conference headed by Saudi Arabia's King Abdullah in 2008 (referred to in Chapter 4), one will find a joint concern for 'preserving the institution of the family and protecting societies from deviant behaviors'.[1] More liberal religionists, however, would rather see Saudi Arabia's harsh regulations against homosexuality as seriously 'deviating' from central human rights principles – and even as 'extreme'.

In general parlance, the term 'extremism' is usually associated with violence and also with 'terrorism'. After the Balkan wars in the 1990s, suicide bombings in Israel, 9/11, and other dramatic terrorist attacks in the following decades (including the terrorist massacre by Anders Behring Breivik on 22 July 2011 and jihadist violence in West-African countries), the term extremism has increasingly been associated with religion. Correspondingly, one will also find characterizations such as 'Christian' or 'Muslim' right-wing-extremism.[2]

Considering other determining factors ranging from politics to psychology, as well as the notoriously difficult distinction between 'religion' and the 'secular', one might legitimately ask 'what's so religious about religious terrorism?' (Gunning and Jackson 2011; cf. Cavanaugh 2009). Mark Juergensmeyer and others are right, however, in saying that religion is important enough as a motivating and mobilizing factor to require separate analyses of 'religious violence' and 'religious extremism'. The question briefly dealt with in this postscript is about what should be counted as extremism in the religious field, and how – according to Christian and Muslim activists – it should be countered.

In Chapter 4, I referred to the so-called London Declaration for Global Peace and Resistance against Extremism[3] which was announced in September 2011 at a 'Peace for Humanity'-conference hosted by the Pakistani-based organization Minhaj ul-Qur'an. The Declaration was launched as a follow-up to a 600-page fatwa against terrorism from 2010 by their leader Muhammad Tahir ul-Qadri.

The signatories to the Declaration 'reject unequivocally all terrorism because at the heart of all religions is a belief in the sanctity of the lives of the innocent'. The Declaration also rejects 'as mistaken and spurious any assertions made by both Muslims and non-Muslims that the world is currently locked in an inexorable struggle between the Islam and the West'. It calls for the removal of conspiracy theories and for international measures aimed at 'de-radicalization of those who might mistakenly believe that their religion tolerates indiscriminate and wanton violence'.

The roots of this important Declaration are found in Pakistan, a country long threatened by extremist violence in the name of religion. But how should 'extremism' be defined in a country like Pakistan? When Tahir ul -Qadri's fatwa against terrorism was launched in Scandinavia, at an anti-radicalism meeting in Copenhagen in September 2012, Tahir ul-Qadri was criticized publicly for having played an active role in shaping Pakistan's anti-blasphemy laws from the 1980s.[4] By making defamation of the Prophet punishable by death and opening an avenue for people to accuse their neighbours of blasphemy, these sections of Pakistan's Penal Code create fear among the country's Muslim and non-Muslim minorities (cf. Chapter 4). If 'terrorism' means spreading fear, the anti-blasphemy laws in Pakistan would clearly be characterized as legalized terror by their victims.

Tahir ul-Qadri may have changed his mind about the anti-blasphemy laws and the way in which they have been practiced since the 1980s.[5] But in the view of the victims, legalized forms of terror (another example would be some countries' harsh legislation against homosexuality, based on Islamic or Christian arguments) cannot be excluded from the discussion of religion and terrorism.

Breivik's extremism: Populist perceptions and hyper-violent performance

Terrorism – as (threats of) violence against innocents – also can not be separated from hate speech against other religions. On 22 July 2011, Norway experienced a bomb attack against the capital's government buildings which killed 8 people, and a shocking massacre which left 69 young people dead and 55 severely injured at a summer camp on the island of Utøya organized by the youth division of the ruling Labour Party. The perpetrator, Anders Behring Breivik, presented himself as a 'cultural Christian', defending Europe by waging war against Muslims and their 'cultural Marxist' (i.e. socialist) accomplices. His 1,500-page manifesto ('2083 – An European Declaration of Independence'), which was launched on the day of terror, is replete which religious imagery, including Paganist references (Asprem 2011). It is also heavily marked by anti-feminist rhetoric (Salomonsen 2013).

From Juergensmeyer's perspective, Breivik's horrendous acts could be characterized as a 'theater of terror' and a form of 'performance violence' (2003: 121ff.). But who did his message reach, apart from the killed, injured and traumatized victims? His deeds were vehemently condemned even by those who, for a large part shared his anti-Islamic or 'counter-jihadist' world view. But his stated *motives* were drawn from anti-Islamic rhetoric rife on both the internet and more conventional parts of the media scene.

At the San Francisco meeting of the American Academy Religion in the autumn of 2011, a seminar dealt with 'Anti-Islamic Populism in the United States'. A key point of reference was the report 'Fear, Inc. The Roots of the Islamophobia Network in America' published a couple of months earlier. The report documented that many proponents of the 'Stop Islamization' and 'creeping Sharia' discourse in US media (including neoconservatives and representatives of the New Christian Right) were cited with approval in Breivik's manifesto. The summary introduction mentions in particular Robert Spencer and Pamela Geller.

Breivik was also inspired by anti-Islamic discourses and activists on the European scene. One of Breivik's favourite blogs, where his ideological inspirator and fellow Norwegian Fjordman had been publishing for years, was the 'Gates of Vienna' – a name which connotes the perennial threat of Muslim invasion in Europe. It has also been documented (Bangstad 2013) how influenced Breivik was by the so-called Eurabia discourse. Its main proponent Bat Ye'or is characterized by Breivik as 'the leading scholar of Islam's expansion and its treatment of non-Muslims' (Breivik 2011: 84).

What is or is not 'extremism', in this landscape of conspiracy theories and hate speech that sometimes (but not necessarily) bleed into physical violence? The same question can be raised about widespread anti-Christian attitudes in parts of the Muslim world that may serve as ideological ammunition for attacks on Christian neighbours (cf. Chapter 4).

With regard to anti-Islamic attitudes in the West, should right-wing *populism* with anti-Islamic and anti-socialist inclinations be seen as an ideological relative of violent *extremism*? Or should the term extremism be reserved for violent movements only?

United against extremism – in the name of God?

In November 2011, some months after the terror in Oslo and at Utøya, the national Contact Group between the Church of Norway and the Islamic Council Norway issued a 'Joint Statement Opposing Religious Extremism'.[6] The group's work on this statement had commenced long before 22 July, and a joint trip to Bosnia and Herzegovina was part of the preparation. The statement refers explicitly to the massacre of Bosnian Muslims in Srebrenica in July 1995; the attacks on the World Trade Centre and Pentagon on 11 September 2001; the terror in Oslo and on Utøya on 22 July 2011; and other examples of religiously motivated terror such as the demolition of the Babri Mosque in Ayodhya, India in December 1992.

The group's statement links the notion of extremism to violence but also includes the use of threats: 'Extremism involves the use of violence, force or threats to promote the extremists' idea'. Further identifying dangerous signs of *religious* extremism, the joint statement seems to envisage a sliding scale which begins with the extremists' conviction 'that they are alone in interpreting their own religion correctly' and may end with the explicit willingness to use violence to enforce their convictions on others who are defined as deadly enemies. On this sliding scale from conviction to violence, the statement also includes the refusal to coexist with certain groups of people, and the language of hate.

Interestingly in the light of both Breivik's anti-feminism and rape as a weapon of war in the Balkan wars, the Christian-Muslim statement also includes religiously motivated violence against women in its broad definition of extremism: 'Extremists use gender-based hierarchies and power structures in which women are denied human rights and human dignity on the same level as men.'

On the basis of this broad definition of religious extremism, the joint statement stresses the need 'to identify and oppose tendencies to religious extremism as early as possible'. It issues a detailed call to Christian and Muslim leaders summoning them to counter any sign of extremist thought and action – in their congregations as well as in public debate. In consonance with the Contact Group's statement from two years before against violence in close relationships,[7] religious leaders, congregations and assemblies are also urged 'to oppose hateful descriptions and harassment of women'. (In the context of Christian-Muslim dialogue, there might not be many other examples of the threat of extremism being so tightly associated with gendered violence.)

In Chapter 3, I noted that documents from Christian-Muslim dialogue in Norway might seem to be moulded in a secular language focused on the ethics of vulnerability and reflecting human rights discourses rather than religious language. The joint statement against extremism more clearly refers to religious discourses, identifying the inherent dangers in forms of religious language that blur the distinction between human and divine goals – with repression of the vulnerable other as a result:

> Religious extremists put themselves in the place of God and believe that they are fighting on behalf of God against the enemies of God. Religious extremism is therefore contrary to the teachings of our religions, especially with respect to the basic dignity and rights of all human beings.

Although formulated as a self-critique on behalf of certain forms of religious language, the passage could also be read as a positive reference to a faith in God which – by confessing *deus semper major* or *allahu akbar* (God is greater) –

puts up a mental barrier against the tendency to identify one's own goals with the will of God. In this perspective, these Christians and Muslims declare, true faith in God may in fact become a protection of the vulnerable other:

> The idea of forcing one's opinions on others is fundamentally opposed to the responsibility and right which we believe that God has given to all human beings, to make their own decisions.

Is extremism part of the religions?

Although the definition of extremism in the Christian-Muslim statement cited above is relatively broad, it is focused on moral and political extremism. It does not address the issue of religious perceptions that might be characterized as extreme solely by virtue of being strongly held or colliding with common scientific knowledge. The latter form of alleged extremism has been characterized as 'descriptive' over against the 'normative' extremism associated with hate speech and violence (see Gule 2012). Against those – among old and new atheists – who would see 'strong faith' in itself as an indicator of extremism, the Christian-Muslim statement from 2011 declares:

> [T]here is no reason to use the term 'religious extremism' for everyone who is strongly committed to his or her faith and who lives out this commitment in different ways. To have a sincere and intense commitment to one's faith has in itself nothing to do with religious extremism, as long as it is combined with respect for the dignity and human rights of others and is not combined with attempts to force the consequences of one's religious or ideological convictions on others.

That is a *normative* statement. The *historical* question of how religion, strong faith and more or less violent extremism have been intertwined is more complicated. For Christians, it may be hard to realize that much of Breivik's anti-Islamic rhetoric, as unfolded in his cut-and-paste manifesto, reflects a relatively-mainstream legacy in European history of seeing Islam as a deadly enemy, constantly competing for control over the same territories that Christians regard as historically theirs.

Tracing the roots of anti-Islamic attitudes in European history, many of the sentiments aired today originate in post-crusade writers such as Petrus

Venerabilis and Thomas Aquinas, seldom referred to as extremists. Among mainstream mediaeval theologians, Islam was seen as a violent religion that was spread by the sword, Muhammad as a womanizing Anti-Christ, and his message as a deliberate perversion of truth (Watt 1991: 85f.). In today's right-wing rhetoric, as found both among 'born again' and 'cultural' Christians, all these elements are replayed, only with the distinct addition of conspiracy theories that suggest that seemingly friendly Muslims only use 'dialogue' as an undercover operation to conquer Europe as claimed by Christian counter-jihadists such as Mark Gabriel (2002; cf. Bangstad 2013 and Chapter 4 above).

Considering these historical facts, should anti-Islamic polemics be referred to as *extreme* phenomena on the fringes of the Christian family, or, rather, are they part of the Christian *mainstream*? Similar questions must be raised with regard to Islamic legacies of stamping the Jewish or Christian other as religiously inferior and subordinate in rights.

Both Christians and Muslims tend to use 'extremism' as a label for those who – from a mainstream perspective – are not regarded as true believers. But the term itself implies that extreme positions are actually *possible* representations of the tradition in question. They may be seen as *extreme* varieties by mainstream theologians. But, from a religious studies perspective, they are representations of the same traditions that 'normal' believers regard as sacred: many of the positions stamped as extreme today may have been seen as perfect normality in previous epochs.

Historically, many of the attitudes condemned today are simply too mainstream to be characterized as extreme. This also means that normative statements against various forms of extremism – in order to be credible – must be underpinned by a self-critical reading not only of the religions' history but also of the sacred scriptures themselves.

Appendices: Three Christian-Muslim Statements

Appendix 1

Joint Declaration on the Freedom of Religion and the Right to Conversion (2007)

Introduction

Since 1993 important processes of interfaith dialogue have taken place between the Islamic Council of Norway and the Church of Norway Council on Ecumenical and International Relations. In this dialogue work, freedom of religion is a core issue.

This ongoing dialogue is based on the fundamental values of mutual respect and trust. Its purpose is to prevent conflicts and to create space for understanding between Muslims and Christians as they relate to each other and to Norwegian society in general. A particular task has been to challenge prejudices and stereotypes in their conceptions of each other and to combat islamophobia and discrimination of the Muslim minority in Norway.

In Norway there are few conversions from Christianity to Islam or vice versa. Nevertheless the two bodies underline that there should be no doubt that freedom of religion, with the right to conversion, is a fully acknowledged principle, reflected in attitudes and accepted in practice, both by the Islamic Council of Norway and the Church of Norway Council on Ecumenical and International Relations.

Joint Declaration

The Islamic Council of Norway and the Church of Norway Council on Ecumenical and International Relations jointly declare that everyone is free to adopt the religious faith of their choice. We denounce, and are committed to counteracting all violence, discrimination and harassment inflicted in reaction to a person's conversion, or desire to convert, from one religion to another, be it in Norway or abroad.

We interpret our religious traditions such that everyone has the right to freely choose their religious belief and faith community, and to practice their religion publicly as well as privately.

Missionary activity and information to others about our faith must be done according to ethically accepted standards, that is, without the use of any form of force or manipulation. If freedom of religion is to be upheld, all conversion must happen freely.

As religious communities we experience joy within our respective contexts whenever a person wishes to share our faith and join our religious community. Therefore we also respect a person's right to convert to a different religion than our own.

Oslo, 22nd of August 2007
Shoaib Sultan, General Secretary Islamic Council of Norway
Olav Fykse Tveit, General Secretary Church of Norway Council on Ecumenical and International Relations

Appendix 2

Say NO to Violence! (2009)

Joint Statement on Violence in the Family and in Close Relationships, by the Islamic Council of Norway and the Church of Norway Council on Ecumenical and International Relations

Introduction

Since 1993 a Contact Group between Islamic Council of Norway and Council on Ecumenical and International Relations of Church of Norway has met to discuss various issues concerning religion and society. The group works for greater understanding between Christians and Muslims and seeks to further the contribution of these religions to the community at large.

For a long time the Contact Group has discussed issues concerning gender and equality. The dialogue has shown that both Christians and Muslims regard human integrity and freedom from violence as fundamental starting points for approaching these issues.

Nevertheless, violence in families and in close relationships is a serious social problem in Norwegian society. Suffice to say that one out of four women is exposed to violence in the family and in close relationships. Therefore, in our capacity as religious communities, we want to contribute positively to the struggle against the violence in family and in close relationships, both by our attitudes and our actions.

Statement

Violence in families and in close relationships is a major social problem in Norway, which occurs at all levels of society and within all religious and cultural communities. It affects both sexes, especially women. Examples of this violence can be intimidation, deprivation of liberty, infringement upon integrity, physical assault, sexual harassment and even rape and murder. Doubtlessly, violence of this kind represents brutal abuses of basic human rights and has destructive consequences for individuals and society.

Violence in families and in close relationships also affects children. Children are either direct victims of physical and non-physical violence or have to suffer its horrors indirectly by being witnesses to violence towards others.

Violence in families and in close relationships is a criminal act which goes against our religious teachings and the human rights. This applies both in Norway and globally.

As Christians and Muslims, we believe that man and woman are created equal, and that none of them has a right to exercise violence against the other. In unambiguous terms we especially denounce violence against women since women are most exposed to domestic violence. We believe that both of our religions can provide sources of inspiration and counsel that can lead to a better life filled with love and mutual respect. We believe that the home should be a safe and pleasant place for children to grow up – without violence. Last but not the least; we strongly condemn any misuse of the teachings of our religions in order to legitimize violence in the family or in close relationships.

Since our human and religious values encourage us to adopt positive principles and ethical responsibility within society we, as Christians and Muslims in Norway, will prevent and resist all shapes and shades of violence in families and in close relationships.

We:

1. encourage our respective congregations/communities to counteract violence in the family and in close relationships and clearly express a position of no tolerance in this area,
2. encourage politicians to put the problem on their agenda and to work for effective political action and no tolerance of violence in the family and in close relationships,

3. appeal to the Norwegian society in general to address this as a common problem and to take part in the struggle against violence in the family and in close relationships.

Oslo, 9th of November 2009
Shoaib M. Sultan, General Secretary, Islamic Council of Norway
Olav Fykse Tveit, General Secretary Church of Norway Council on Ecumenical and International Relations

Appendix 3

Joint Statement Opposing Religious Extremism

By the Islamic Council of Norway and the Church of Norway Council on Ecumenical and International Relations

Religious extremism

Religious extremism has various and alarming results. The world community has witnessed tragedies such as the demolition of the Babri Mosque in Ayodhya, India in December 1992 and the violence that followed, the massacre of Bosnian Muslims in Srebrenica in July 1995, the aircraft that were flown into the World Trade Centre and Pentagon on 11th September 2001 and the terror in Oslo and on Utøya 22nd July 2011. Religious extremism is part of the global reality. But religious extremism also threatens the life, welfare and rights of human beings in many local situations and in many ways, without being given the same attention as these vast tragedies, for example by religiously legitimized violence in close relationships, the desecration of holy places and threats to those who take part in public debates. Whatever the extent, we cannot accept that individuals or groups in various ways are made the victims of religious extremism.

Extremism involves the use of violence, force or threats to promote the extremists' ideal society or to attack individuals or groups. This often happens without religion being involved. But some use religion or religious rhetoric to explain or justify extremism, for example by interpreting religious writings so that they seem to support extremist attitudes and actions. This is what we mean by religious extremism, which we as religious leaders have a special responsibility to oppose.

Characteristics

Religious extremism has many characteristics. We mention especially these:

- Extremists believe that they are alone in interpreting their own religion correctly, so that they cannot cooperate with others who think differently, even though these belong to the same religious tradition.
- Extremists are convinced that there are groups of people that it is impossible to coexist with, and which they must therefore oppose or remove, either from society as a whole or from certain places or areas.
- Extremists reduce human dignity for groups that they oppose, and reject the idea that human rights apply to these groups.
- Extremists accuse those who think differently of having certain political, ethical or religious opinions, without allowing them to define for themselves who they are or what they believe.
- Extremists use gender-based hierarchies and power structures in which women are denied human rights and human dignity on the same level as men.
- Extremists use a language of hate, inciting to conflict with certain groups of people and with those who disagree with their convictions.
- Extremists are willing to use terror, violence or other forms of compulsion in order to enforce the consequences of their religious views on others.

This is not intended to be a complete list, but includes what we think are important characteristics of religious extremism. The more of these characteristics that are present in a specific case, the more serious it is. Each of these characteristics can be present with different degrees of seriousness. We therefore believe that it is important to identify and oppose tendencies to religious extremism as early as possible.

With this in mind, it is also clear that there is no reason to use the term 'religious extremism' for everyone who is strongly committed to his or her faith and who lives out this commitment in different ways. To have a sincere and intense commitment to one's faith has in itself nothing to do with religious extremism, as long as it is combined with respect for the dignity and human rights of others and is not combined with attempts to force the consequences of one's religious or ideological convictions on others.

Joint appeal

The Islamic Council of Norway and the Church of Norway Council on Ecumenical and International Relations reject all forms of religious extremism. Religious extremists put themselves in the place of God and believe that they are fighting on behalf of God against the enemies of God. Religious extremism is therefore contrary to the teachings of our religions, especially with respect to the basic dignity and rights of all human beings. The idea of forcing one's opinions on others is fundamentally opposed to the responsibility and right which we believe that God has given to all human beings, to make their own decisions. To live in peace and reconciliation with one another across the boundaries of culture and religion is in fundamental harmony with the basic values of our religions.

The Islamic Council of Norway and the Church of Norway Council on Ecumenical and International Relations are especially concerned that possible tendencies to religious extremism in our own ranks should come to light. We therefore urge Muslims and Christians to prevent and oppose all forms of religious extremism both in their respective communities and in their fellowship with one another.

- We urge religious leaders to continue to raise these questions in their preaching and teaching, order to reject and prevent extremism in their own ranks.
- We urge religious leaders and faith communities to join together and speak out publicly against religious extremism.
- We urge religious leaders and faith communities to develop contingency plans to prevent and oppose extremism.
- We urge congregations and assemblies to raise these issues in study groups, plenary sessions and dialogues.
- We urge religious leaders, congregations and assemblies to protect one another's members, holy places and other institutions which could be threatened by religious extremists.

- We urge religious leaders, congregations and assemblies to expose and oppose the use of holy writings and religious rhetoric in a way that can create conditions for the development of religious extremism.
- We urge religious leaders, congregations and assemblies to speak out against hateful and threatening descriptions of others, not least in the media and on the internet.
- We urge religious leaders, congregations and assemblies to oppose hateful descriptions and harassment of women.
- We urge the media and other public bodies to present a nuanced picture of religious belief when violence and force are committed in the name of religion.
- We urge the various faith communities to use their international contacts and networks to strengthen the struggle against religious extremism nationally and internationally.

Oslo, 22nd November 2011

Mehtab Afsar, General Secretary Islamic Council of Norway

Berit Hagen Agøy, General Secretary, Church of Norway Council on Ecumenical and International Relations

Notes

Chapter 1

1 <http://faber.whiteheadresearch.org/theme-transrel-disc.html> [accessed 18.07.13], cf. Faber 2003. Roland Faber goes on by defining 'transreligious discourse' as follows: 'Theoretically, it studies the possibility of such a transfer, not by comparison but by following the trajectories of mutual influences and traces of one religion (way of life, doctrine, or ritual) in the other or by examining their reflection in diverse theologies. Practically, it studies matters and ways of transfer.'

2 Cf. Paul Hedges: 'While many involved may come from one particular background, Interreligious Studies involves the recognition that as a subject area it interacts with many disciplines and areas of life and study' (Hedges 2013: 1077).

Chapter 2

1 A version of this chapter was first published in the journal *Approaching Religion* (Leirvik 2011b).

2 See for instance Atterton, Calarco, and Friedman 2004 and Illman 2006.

3 I had my first experiences in Christian-Muslim dialogue when working as a Lutheran pastor in an inner city congregation in Oslo (from the late 1980s) and worked subsequently full time with interfaith dialogue in the church-related Emmaus Centre for Dialogue and Spirituality (until 1996).

4 At the Faculty of Theology, University of Oslo (from 1996).

5 <http://folk.uio.no/leirvik/Kontaktgruppa.htm>

6 <www.trooglivssyn.no>

7 An early Norwegian example would be a newspaper article from 2005 by the then Minister of Municipal and Regional Affairs Erna Solberg, with the heading 'Dialogue with religious milieus' ('Dialog med religiøse miljøer', *Vårt Land*, 12 July 2005). The article should probably be read in light of an interview with Solberg two years before, in which she (after a conversation with the British Minister of Inclusion) encouraged Norwegian Muslims to modernize their Islam ('Solberg utfordrer norske muslimer', *Aftenposten*, 4 November 2003).

8 A Norwegian example of how the notion 'dialogue' is embedded in discourses of securitization can be found in the Ministry of Justice and the Police's plan from 2010 'to prevent radicalization and violent extremism' (Justis- og politidepartementet: 'Felles trygghet – felles ansvar. Handlingsplan for å forebygge radikalisering og voldelig ekstremisme', pp. 24 and 32).

9 'The meaning of the utterance is quite literally neither the one nor the other' (Bhabha 2004: 56).

10 In an article about an interreligious dialogue group in Malmö, Sweden, Anne Sofie Roald demonstrates how much the agenda of this group reflected established social-ethical topics in Christian-ecumenical dialogue. She also notes a slight frustration among the Muslim participants that topics that were felt to be at odds with a liberal Christian agenda, such as heaven and hell or alcohol consumption, were never included in the group's agenda (Roald 2002).

11 <www.jus.uio.no/smr/english/about/programmes/oslocoalition/>

12 <www.kirken.no/?event=showNews&FamID=93378> [accessed 18.07.13].

13 <http://irn.no/2006/index.php?option=com_content&task=view&id=265&Itemid=39> [accessed 18.07.13].

14 See Appendix 1 and <www.kirken.no/?event=showNews&FamID=101461> [accessed 18.07.13].

15 See Appendix 2 and <www.kirken.no/?event=showNews&FamID=17453> [accessed 18.07.13].

16 <http://www.udir.no/kl06/RLE1-01/> [accessed 18.07.13].

17 KUF (Ministry of Education and Research)/Nasjonalt læremiddelsenter: *Veiledning til lærplanverket for den 10-årige grunnskolen (L97): Kristendomskunnskap med religions- og livssynsopplæring*, paragraph 3.4.2.

Chapter 3

1 <www.acommonword.com>

2 '. . . the change I want to define and trace is one which takes us from a society in which it was virtually impossible not to believe in God, to one in which faith, even for the staunchest believer, is one human possibility among others' (Taylor 2007: 3).

3 Searches in the Norwegian media archive Atekst (all types of sources) return 5 hits between 1985 and 1996, 39 hits from 1997 to 2002 and as many as 459 hits from 2003–9.

4 'Frykter religionsblanding', *Vårt Land*, 17 December 1992.

5 'Felles front mot rasisme og partnerskapsloven', *Vårt Land*, 17 December 1992.

6 Olav Fykse Tveit: 'Felles samtale, ikkje felles front', *Vårt Land*, 19 December 1992.

7 See for example Nina Witoszek: 'Å snakke om det' (*Dagbladet*, 12 February 2005); Knut Olav Åmås: 'Konflikt er normalt, ikke galt' (*Aftenposten*, 15 January 2007); Sarah Azmeh Rasmussen: 'Dialog som en blindvei' (*Aftenposten*, 22 January 2007); Jens Tomas Anfindsen: 'Kirkens dialogatleter' (*Vårt Land*, 26 April 2007); 'Bekkemellem lei av dialog og toleranse' (*Vårt Land*, 3 March 2009).

8 *Magazinet*, 10 January 2006, p. 2.

9 See Jonas Gahr Støre: 'Dialog som prosjekt', *Dagsavisen*, 10 March 2006, published also on the government's home page.

10 Cf. a debate in the Christian daily *Vårt Land* after the delegation trips, between Jens Tomas Anfindsen ('Ut på tur, aldri sur' og 'Rot fra Mellomkirkelig råd', *Vårt Land*, 20 February and 6 March 2006) and Vebjørn Horsfjord ('Dialog og delegasjonsreise' og 'Mellomkirkelig råd og dialog', *Vårt Land*, 22 February and 8 March 2006).

11 Cf. the debate in *Klassekampen* in 2009 between Jill Loga ('Offentlig utenomsnakk. Om den rosa elefanten i dagens religionsdebatter' and 'Liberal dialog på noens bekostning?' *Klassekampen*, 15 and 24 October 2009) and Anne Hege Grung/Oddbjørn Leirvik ('Den liberale religionsdialogen' and 'Sensitive tema i religionsdialogen', *Klassekampen*, 20 and 28 October 2009).

12 Cf. the interesting critique by Sharam Alghasi in the newspaper article 'Norges nye "vi"', *Aftenposten*, 14 May 2008.

13 'Skjebnevalg for Norge? Åpent brev fra kristne og muslimske ledere om kjønnsnøytral ekteskapslov', *Norge IDAG*, 11 June 2005.

14 'Islamsk-kristen allianse påvirker FN', *Vårt Land*, 20 June 2002.

15 The idea of an overlapping consensus was already formulated in Rawls' *A Theory of Justice* (Rawls 1999, first edition 1972) and later developed in his book *Political Liberalism* (Rawls 2005, first edition 1993).

16 'Stopp volden mot kristne i Pakistan', kirken.no 13 August 2009 <www.kirken.no/?event=showNews&FamID=93378> [accessed 18.07.13].

17 See Appendix 1 and <www.kirken.no/english/news.cfm?artid=149142> [accessed 18.07.13].

18 Cf. the book title by Amina Wadud (2006): *Inside the Gender Jihad: Women's Reform in Islam.*

19 See Appendix 2 and <www.kirken.no/english/doc/engelsk/Joint_declaration_violence_relations_0911.pdf> [accessed 18.07.13].

Chapter 4

1 Cf. Lena Larsen: 'Striden om Muhammad', *Dagbladet*, 13 February 2010.

2 Cf. Jan Opsal: 'Karikaturen av den andre', *Stavanger Aftenblad*, 6 October 2012.

3 'God, the god, it's long way there, a road that goes via the Other' (Levinas 1993: 215, my translation).
4 'Unfavorable Views of Both Jews and Muslims Increase in Europe', Pew Global Attitudes Project, 17 September 2008, <http://pewresearch.org/pubs/955/unfavorable-views-of-both-jews-and-muslims-increase-in-europe> [accessed 18.07.13].
5 'Islamic Extremism: Common Concern for Muslim and Western Publics', Pew Global Attitudes Project, 14 July 2005, <www.pewglobal.org/2005/07/14/islamic-extremism-common-concern-for-muslim-and-western-publics/> [accessed 18.07.13].
6 'The Great Divide: How Westerners and Muslims View Each Other', Pew Global Attitudes Project, 22 June 2006, <www.pewglobal.org/2006/06/22/the-great-divide-how-westerners-and-muslims-view-each-other/> [accessed 18.07.13].
7 Same survey.
8 <www.londondeclaration.com/> [accessed 18.07.13].
9 'Ønsket konflikt med islam', *Aftenposten*, 31 January 2006.
10 More recent titles of Mark A. Gabriel include *Journey into the Mind of an Islamic Terrorist* (2006) and *Culture Clash: Islam's War on the West* (2007).
11 *Mot målet* 5: 2003 (my translation).
12 Oddbjørn Leirvik: 'Boka Hagen har lest', *Dagbladet*, 20 November 2004.
13 'Lovpriste Israel, angrep islam' (*Bergens Tidende*, 14 July 2004). Cf. Hagen 2007: 466–70.
14 My translation ('. . . krigsherren, voldsmannen og kvinnemishandleren Muhammed som myrdet og aksepterte voldtekt som erobringsteknikk').
15 <www.carm.org/islam/Jesus_Muhammad.htm> [accessed 18.07.13].
16 'Muslim Publics Divided on Hamas and Hezbollah', Pew Global Attitudes Project, 2 December 2010, <www.pewglobal.org/2010/12/02/muslims-around-the-world-divided-on-hamas-and-hezbollah/> [accessed 18.07.13].
17 <www.pewforum.org/Muslim/the-worlds-muslims-religion-politics-society-beliefs-about-sharia.aspx> [accessed 18.07.13].
18 'An International call for Moratorium on Corporal Punishment, Stoning and the Death Penalty in the Islamic World', 5 April 2005, <www.tariqramadan.com/spip.php?article264> [accessed 18.07.13].

Chapter 5

1 <www.crihl.org/>
2 'The participants affirm the following principles: . . . (5) Respecting heavenly religions, preserving their high status, condemning any insult to their

symbols, and combating the exploitation of religion in the instigation of racial discrimination . . . (7) The significance of religion and moral values and the need for humans to revert to their Creator in their fight against crime, corruption, drugs, and terrorism, and in preserving the institution of the family and protecting societies from deviant behaviors . . . (8) The family is the basic unit of society and its nucleus. Protecting it from disintegration is a cornerstone for any secure and stable society.' See <http://interfaithorganisations.net/2008/07/28/the-madrid-declaration-issued-by-the-world-conference-on-dialogue/> [accessed 18.07.13].

3 See discussion of these issues with reference to the Norwegian context, in the State Report NOU 2013: 1, chapter 23.

Chapter 6

1 This chapter constitutes an updated version of 'Tolerance, Conscience and Solidarity: Globalized Concepts in Ethical and Religious Education', published in Sturla J. Stålsett (ed.) *Religion in a Globalised Age: Transfers and Transformations, Integration and Resistance.* Oslo: Novus 2008, pp. 105–16.

2 Cf. the original French title of his book *Les identités meurtrières.*

3 <www.un-documents.net/dpt.htm> [accessed 18.07.13].

4 See the project's website, <www.jus.uio.no/smr/english/about/programmes/oslocoalition/tolerance/> [accessed 18.07.13].

5 <http://theamericanmuslim.org/tam.php/features/articles/the_spirit_of_tolerance_in_islam/> [accessed 18.07.13].

6 Cited from an earlier US website about 'Bridges of Tolerance', <www.usinfo.pl/krakow/tolerance> [accessed 12.11.08].

7 In 2002, Khaled Abou El Fadl (with Tariq Ali, Milton Viorst, John Esposito and Others) published an essay on *The Place of Tolerance in Islam* (Fadl et al. 2002).

8 Oxford English Dictionary, web-edition (<http://dictionary.oed.com/>, entrance 'Tolerance'.

9 The Latin title is *Epistola de Tolerantia* (1685).

10 Cf. the listed meanings of *tasamuh* in an Islamic dictionary of Islamic terms at <www.islamicresources.com/> [accessed 12.11.08]: 'forbearance, indulgence, tolerance, forgiveness'.

11 <www.tokohosting.com/icis/content.php?aksi=latar_belakang&lang=english> [accessed 12.11.08].

12 Chinese and Japanese translations of the Declaration, however, reflect the fact that in standard usage it is rather the word *ryoshin* – which means 'the good heart' – that has been chosen for conscience.

13 The New Testament reference is Matthew 7.12: 'So whatever you wish that others would do to you, do also to them, for this is the Law and the Prophets.'

14 In the Jewish Bible, one finds the injunction to love one's neighbour as oneself in Leviticus 19.18. In the New Testament, the injunction occurs as a fixed formula both in the Gospels (Mt. 22.39f. and Mk 12.31), in Paul (Rom. 13.8f. and Gal. 5.14) and in the Epistle of James (Jam 2.8).

15 *Al-qiyam wa-l-akhlaq*, First, Second and Third Grade (2001–2). Cf. Kouchok 2007 and Pink 2003.

16 *Al-qiyam wa-l-akhlaq*, Second Grade, Part Two (2001–2), p. 1.

17 For instance in *Kitab al-qiyam wa-l-akhlaq* (2002–3), Fourth Grade, one will find seven references to the Qur'an, one reference to Hadith and a single reference to the Bible.

18 'Badr [Then Minister of Education] Announces Return of the Ethics Subject in Schools', *Misr Gedida*, 4 April 2010, <www.masress.com/misrelgdida/26014> [accessed 18.07.13].

19 *Al-tarbiya al-diniyya al-masihiyya*, Fifth Grade, Part One (2001–2), 13. Cf. Acts 7. 51–53.

20 *Al-tarbiya al-diniyya al-'islamiyya*, Fourth Grade, Part One (2002–3), 33.

21 *Al-tarbiya al-diniyya al-'islamiyya*, Fourth Grade, Part Two (2002–3), 4.

22 Oxford English Dictionary, web-edition <http://dictionary.oed.com/>, entrance 'Solidarity'.

Chapter 7

1 A previous version of this chapter was published in David Cheetham, Ulrich Winkler, Oddbjørn Leirvik and Judith Gruber (eds) *Interreligious Hermeneutics in Pluralistic Europe. Between Texts and People.* Amsterdam and New York: Rodopi 2011, pp. 333–53.

Chapter 8

1 Cf. 22: 67–9: 'To every People have We appointed rites and ceremonies which they must follow . . . Allah will judge between you on the Day of Judgement concerning the matters in which Ye differ.'

2 Cf. Zebiri 1997: 20, 28.

3 Implying that Jews and Christian have altered their scriptures. Cf. Muslim-Christian Research Group 1989: 78–81 and Zebiri 1997: 50ff.

4 Cf. his book-title *Inter Religion* (Askari 1977).

5 'There was . . . arrogance and passion for power, justified with reference to the elevation and lordship of Christ, in a demand to partake in it.' Schumann 1988: 173, my translation (. . . 'es gab . . . Arroganz und Herrschsucht, die sich mit dem Hinweis auf die Erhöhung und Herrschaft Christi rechtfertigte und beanspruchte, an ihnen Anteil zu haben').

6 My translation. ('Denn nur am Kreuz, durch die endliche Überwindung des Eigenwillens und seines Zieles, "zu sein wie Gott", kann die immer wieder neue menschliche Versuchung zum "*širk*" µberwunden werden.')

7 My translation. ('Jesu Abwehr einer Identifizierung des Gottesherrschaft mit einem politischen Gesellschafts- oder Staatsverständnis wird von Christen nicht als Mangel verstanden, sondern ihre Vermischung gerade als unheilige Versuchung.')

8 My translation. Cf. Emmanuel Levinas' reflections on the face of the Other as an epiphany of God in his book *Of God Who Comes to Mind* (1998).

9 <www.acommonword.com>

10 <http://onetruename.com/Rumi.htm> [accessed 18.07.13].

11 *Sahih Muslim*, Book 032, Number 6232: 'Merit of visiting the sick' (in the translation of Mahmoud Matraji). Beyrouth: Dar El Fiker 1993, Vol. IVa: 176.

12 *De rettvises hager. Al-Nawawis samling av overleveringer om profeten Muhammad.* Translated by Nora S. Eggen. Oslo: Bokklubben 2008.

13 'An International Call for Moratorium on Corporal Punishment, Stoning and the Death Penalty in the Islamic World', 5 April 2005, <www.tariqramadan.com/spip.php?article264> [accessed 18.07.13].

14 'Liv er helligere enn Koranen', *Klassekampen* 4 April 2011 (my translation).

15 Bushra Ishaq: 'Muslimer i endring' ('Muslims in the process of change'), *Aftenposten*, 5 September 2009 (my translation).

Chapter 10

1 <http://interfaithorganisations.net/2008/07/28/the-madrid-declaration-issued-by-the-world-conference-on-dialogue/> (point 8) [accessed 18.07.13].

2 Cf. Shoiab Sultan: 'Muslimske høyreekstremister?', nrk.no 5 February 2013, <www.nrk.no/ytring/muslimske-hoyreekstremister_-1.10898585> [accessed 18.07.13].

3 <www.londondeclaration.com/>

4 'Minister cancels appearance at anti-radicalism conference', *The Copenhagen Post*, 6 September 2012, <http://cphpost.dk/news/national/minister-cancels-appearance-anti-radicalism-conference> [accessed 18.07.13].

5 'I have many reservations on Blasphemy Law: Tahir-ul-Qadri', *News Pakistan*, 7 September 2012, <www.newspakistan.pk/2012/09/07/reservations-blasphemy-law-tahir-ul-qadri/> [accessed 18.07.13].
6 See Appendix 3 and <www.kirken.no/english/doc/engelsk/religious_Extremism2_nov2011.pdf>
7 See Appendix 2.

Bibliography

Abou El Fadl, Khaled (2001) *Speaking in God's Name. Islamic Law, Authority, and Women.* Oxford: Oneworld.

— (2002) *The Place of Tolerance in Islam*. Boston: Beacon Press.

Ahlstrand, Kajsa (2003) Softening in Inter-faith Discourse. Emmaus Centre for Dialogue and Spirituality. <http://emmausnett.no/ressurser/ahlstrand_softening.shtml> [accessed 8.01.2013].

al-'Aqqad, A. M. (n.d.) *'Abqariyyat al-Masih*. First edition: 1953. Cairo: Dar nahdat Misr.

Ali, Wajahat et al. (2011) *Fear, Inc. The Roots of the Islamophobia Network in America.* Center for American Progress.

Amir-Moazami, Schirin (2011) 'Pitfalls of Consensus-orientated Dialogue: The German Islam Conference' (Deutsche Islam Konferenz). *Approaching Religion* 1 (1), 2–15.

an-Na'im, Abdullahi Ahmed (1990) *Toward an Islamic Reformation. Civil Liberties, Human Rights, and International Law*. Syracuse, NY: Syracuse University Press.

Appleby, R. Scott (1998) *Religion and Global Affairs. Religious 'Militants for Peace'. SAIS Review* 18 (2), 38–44.

— (1999) *The Ambivalence of the Sacred: Religion, Violence, and Reconciliation.* Lanham, MD: Rowman & Littlefield.

Asinor, Charles (2006) 'Religious Identity and its Potential for Violent Conflicts. A Ghanian Perspective'. Master thesis in Intercontextual Theology, Faculty of Theology, University of Oslo.

Askari, Hasan (1972) 'The Dialogical Relationship between Christianity and Islam'. *Journal of Ecumenical Studies* 9, 477–87.

— (1977) *Inter-religion. A Collection of Essays.* Aligarh, India: Printwell Publications.

Asprem, Egil (2011) 'The Birth of Counterjihadist Terrorism: Reflections on some Unspoken Dimensions of 22 July 2011'. *The Pomegranate: Journal of Contemporary Paganist Studies* 13 (1), 17–32.

Atterton, Peter, Calarco, Matthew and Friedman, Maurice S. (2004) *Levinas & Buber. Dialogue & Difference*. Pittsburgh, PA: Duquesne University Press.

Balchin, Cassandra (2011) 'Religion and Development. A Practitioner's Perspective on Instrumentalisation'. *The Institute of Development Studies Bulletin* 42 (1), 15–20.

Bangstad, Sindre (2013) 'Eurabia Comes to Norway'. *Islam and Christian-Muslim Relations*. Pre-published online, June 2013 http://dx.doi.org/10.1080/09596410.2013.783969.

Barnes, Michael (2002) *Theology and the Dialogue of Religions*. Cambridge: Cambridge University Press.

Beauvoir, Simone de (2010) *The Second Sex*. New York: Knopf.

Benard, C. (2003) *Civil Democratic Islam. Partners, Resources and Strategies*. Santa Monica, CA: RAND Corporation.

Benhabib, Seyla (1992) *Situating the Self: Gender, Community, and Postmodernism in Contemporary Ethics*. Cambridge: Polity Press.

Berg Eriksen, Trond, Harket, Håkon and Lorenz, Einhart (2005) *Jødehat. Antisemittismens historie fra antikken til i dag*. Oslo: Damm.

Beyer, Peter (2006) *Religions in Global Society*. London and New York: Routledge.

Bhabha, Homi (2004) *The Location of Culture*. London: Routledge.

Borchgrevink, Tordis (2004) 'Globalizing Secularity? Human Rights between Belief and the Pragmatics of Civility', in Sturla J. Stålsett and Oddbjørn Leirvik (eds) *The Power of Faith in Global Politics*. Oslo: Novus, pp. 56–69.

Breidlid, Halldis and Tove Nicolaisen (2011) *I begynnelsen var fortellingen*. Oslo: Universitetsforlaget.

Breivik, Anders Behring [*aka* Berwick, Andrew] (2011) '2083 – A European Declaration of Independence'. Published online.

Brekke, Torkel (2004) 'Religious Nationalism in Contemporary Norway', in Sturla J. Stålsett and Oddbjørn Leirvik (eds) *The Power of Faiths in Global Politics*. Oslo: Novus Press, pp. 117–26.

Bruun, Arvild J. S. (2008) 'Europeisk islam – en studie av norske bosnieres forhold til religion'. Master thesis in Religion and Society, Faculty of Theology, University of Oslo.

Buber, Martin (1987) *I and Thou*. Edinburgh: T&T Clark.

— (1988) *Exclipse of God. Studies in the Relation between Religion and Philosophy*. Atlantic Highlands, NJ: Humanities Press International.

— (2002) *Between Man and Man. With an Introduction by Maurice Friedman*. Translated by R. G. Smith. London and New York: Routledge.

Bunzl, Matti (2007) *Anti-semitism and Islamophobia: Hatreds Old and New in Europe*. Chicago: Chicago University Press.

Buruma, Ian and Margalit, Avishai (2004) *Occidentalism: The West in the Eyes of Its Enemies*. New York: Penguin Press.

Butler, Jennifer S. (2006) *Born Again. The Christian Right Globalized*. London and Ann Arbor, MI: Pluto Press.

Cavanaugh, William T. (2009) *The Myth of Religious Violence: Secular Ideology and the Roots of Modern Conflict*. New York: Oxford University Press.

Cheetham, David (2005) 'The University and Interfaith Education'. *Studies in Interreligious Dialogue* 15 (1), 16–35.

— (2013) *Ways of Meeting and the Theology of Religions*. Farnham: Ashgate.

Cheetham, David, Winkler, Ulrich, Leirvik, Oddbjørn and Gruber, Judith (eds) (2011) *Interreligious Hermeneutics in Pluralistic Europe. Between Texts and People*. Amsterdam and New York: Rodopi.

Christensen, Elise G. (2010) 'Fremstillinger av den Andre i en norsk-muslimsk kontekst. En analyse av Islamic Cultural Centre Norways moskélitteratur og nettsider'. Master thesis in Religion and Society, Faculty of Theology, University of Oslo.

Cobb, John B. (1982) *Beyond Dialogue. Toward a Mutual Transformation of Christianity and Buddhism*. Philadelphia: Fortress Press.

Cornille, Catherine (2008) *The Im-Possibility of Interreligious Dialogue*. New York: The Crossroad Publishing Company.

Cornille, Catherine (ed.) (2013) *The Wiley-Blackwell Companion to Inter-Religious Dialogue*. Chichester: Wiley-Blackwell.

Cornille, Catherine and Conway, Christopher (eds) (2010) *Interreligious Hermeneutics*. Eugene, OR: Cascade Books.

Coward, Harold (2000) *Pluralism in the World Religions. A Short Introduction*. Oxford: Oneworld.

D'Costa, Gavin (1998) 'Theology and Religious Studies in a Pluralist Society: Towards a New Interdisciplinary Identity?' *Norsk Teologisk Tidsskrift* 99 (1), 19–29.

Drees, Willem B. and van Koningsveld, Pieter Sjord (2008) *The Study of Religion and the Training of Muslim Clergy in Europe. Academic and Religious Freedom in the 21st Century*. Leiden: University of Leiden Press.

Dunbar, Scott Daniel (1998) 'The Place of Interreligious Dialogue in the Academic Study of Religion'. *Journal of Ecumenical Studies* 35 (3–4), 455–70.

Dupuis, Jacques (1997) *Toward a Christian Theology of Religious Pluralism*. New York: Orbis Books.

Dussel, E. (2004) 'Deconstruction of the Concept of Tolerance: From Intolerance to Solidarity'. *Constellations* 11(3), 326–33.

Døving, Cora Alexa (2010) 'Anti-Semitism and Islamophobia: A Comparison of Imposed Group Identities'. *Tidsskrift for Islamforskning* (2), 52–76.

— (2012) 'Religionens omveier – det sekulære argument i hijabdebattene', in Sindre Bangstad, Oddbjørn Leirvik and Ingvill Thorson Plesner (eds) *Sekularisme – med norske briller*. Oslo: Unipub, pp. 25–46.

ECRL (2011) *European Council of Religious Leaders Moscow Declaration on Advancing Human Dignity Through Human Rights and Traditional Values*. Oslo: ECRL.

Egnell, Helene (2011) 'Scriptural Reasoning: A Feminist Response', in David Cheetham, Ulrich Winkler, Oddbjørn Leirvik and Judith Gruber (eds) *Interreligious Hermeneutics in Pluralistic Europe. Between Texts and People*. Amsterdam and New York: Rodopi, pp. 333–53.

Eidsvåg, Inge and Larsen, Lena (eds) (1997) *Religion, livssyn og menneskerettigheter I Norge*. Oslo: Universitetsforlaget.

Eidsvåg, Inge and Leirvik, Oddbjørn (eds) (1993) *Fellesskapsetikk i et flerkulturelt Norge*. Oslo: Universitetsforlaget.

Elgvin, Olav (2011) *Secularists, Democratic Islamists and Utopian Dreamers. How Muslim Religious Leaders in Norway Fit Islam into the Norwegian Political System*. Master thesis in Peace and Conflict Studies, University of Oslo. Also published by Lap Lambert Academic Publishing 2012.

Eriksen, Jens Martin and Stjernfelt, Frederik (2009) *Atskillelsens politikk. Multikulturalisme – ideologi og virkelighet*. Oslo: Forlaget Press.

Esack, Farid (1997) *Qur'an, Liberation & Pluralism: An Islamic Perspective of Interreligious Solidarity Against Oppression*. Oxford: Oneworld.

Etikpah, Samuel (2010) 'Interreligious Relations: The Potency of Peaceful Coexistence for Community Development in Rural Ghana'. Master thesis in Intercontextual Theology, Faculty of Theology, University of Oslo.

Faber, Roland (2003) 'Der transreligiöse Diskurs. Zu einer Theologie transformativer Prozesse'. *Polylog. Zeitschrift für interkulturelles Philosophieren* 9, 65–94.

Feuerbach, L. (1960a) *Schriften zur Ethik und nachgelassene Aphorismen. Sämtliche Werke*. Stuttgart: Frommann Verlag Günther Holzboog.

— (1960b) *Theogonie nach den Quellen des classischen, hebräischen und christlichen Altherthums. Sämtliche Werke*. Stuttgart: Frommann Verlag Günther Holzboog.

Fiorenza, Elisabeth Schüssler (1988) 'The Ethics of Biblical Interpretation'. *Journal of Biblical Literature* 107 (1), 3–17.

Fletcher, Jeannine Hill (2013) 'Women in Inter-Religious Dialogue', in Catherine Cornille (ed.) *The Wiley-Blackwell Companion to Inter-Religious Dialogue*. Chichester: Wiley Blackwell, pp. 168–83.

Flood, Gavin (1999) *Beyond Phenomenology. Rethinking the Study of Religion*. London: Cassell.

Ford, David (2006) 'An Interfaith Wisdom: Scriptural Reasoning between Jews, Christians and Muslims', in D. Ford and C. C. Pecknold (eds) *The Promise of Scriptural Reasoning*. Oxford etc.: Blackwell Publishing.

Ford, David and Pecknold, C. C. (eds) (2006) *The Promise of Scriptural Reasoning*. Oxford etc.: Blackwell Publishing.

Frederiks, Martha (2005) 'Hermeneutics from an Inter-religious Perspective?' *Exchange* 9 (2), 102–10.

Freire, Paolo (2003) *De undertryktes pedagogikk*. Oslo: De norske bokklubbene.

Fritsch-Oppermann, Sybille (2003) 'Christian Existence in a Buddhist Context. The Theology of Yagi as a Contribution to an Interreligious Hermeneutics of the "Other"'. *Studies in Interreligious Dialogue* 13 (2), 215–39.

Frydenlund, Iselin (2013) 'Religion, Civility and Conflict: Towards a Concept of Critical Civility'. *Studies in Interreligious Dialogue* 23 (1), 109–24.

Gabriel, Mark (2002) *Islam and Terrorism. What the Qur'an Really Teaches about Christianity, Violence and the Goals of the Islamic Jihad*. Lake Mary, FL: Charisma House.

— (2003) *Islam and the Jews. The Unfinished Battle*. Lake Mary, FL: Charisma House.

— (2004) *Jesus and Muhammad: Profound Differences and Surprising Similarities*. Florida: Charisma House/FrontLine.

Gandhi, Mahatma (1946) *The Mind of Mahatma Gandhi. Compiled by R.K. Prabhu and U.R. Rao*. Madras: Geoffrey Cumberlege, Oxford University Press.

Gerle, Elisabeth (1995) *In Search for a Global Ethics. Theological, Political, and Feminist Perspectives Based on a Critical Analysis of JPIC and WOMP*. Lund: Lund University Press.

Gilje, Nils (2009) 'Filosofisk teologi og religiøs erfaring, et kantiansk perspektiv', in *Religion og kultur. Ein fleirfagleg samtale*. Oslo: Universitetsforlaget, pp. 60–75.

Gorski, Philip S. and Altınordu, Ates (2008) 'After Secularization?' *Annual Review of Sociology* 34, 55–85.

Group, Muslim-Christian Research (1989) *The Challenge of the Scriptures. The Bible and the Qur'an, Faith Meets Faith*. Maryknoll, NY: Orbis.

Grung, Anne Hege (2005) 'Begrepet dialog i Emmaus. Noen refleksjoner om bruken avbegrepet på grunnlag av erfaringer i et flerreligiøst landskap'. *Kirke og Kultur* 110 (1), 87–94.

— (2008) 'Including Gender Perspective in Muslim-Christian Dialogue in Europe and Scandinavia - a Disturbance to Bridge-building or a Contextual Necessity?' in T. Engelsviken, Ernst Harbakk, Rolv Olsen and Thor Strandenæs (eds) *Mission to the World. Communicating the Gospel in the 21st Century. Essays in Honour of Knud Jørgensen*. Oxford: Regnum, pp. 289–97.

— (2011a) *Gender Justice in Christian-Muslims Readings. Christian and Muslim Women in Norway Making Meaning of Texts from the Bible, the Koran, and the Hadith*. Oslo: Unipub.

— (2011b) 'Interreligious Dialogue: Moving between Compartmentalization and Complexity'. *Approaching Religion* 1 (1), 25–32.

Grung, Anne Hege and Larsen, Lena (2000) *Dialog med og uten slør*. Oslo: Pax.

Grødum, Linda (1999) 'Dialogue without Words. The Interaction of Giving and Receiving Massage'. Mag. art. Dissertation, Institute of Sociology, University of Oslo.

Gule, Lars (2012) *Ekstremismens kjennetegn. Ansvar og motsvar*. Oslo: Spartacus.

Gunning, Jeroen and Richard Jackson (2011) 'What's So "Religious" About "Religious Terrorism?"' *Critical Studies on Terrorism* 4 (3), 339–88.

Habermas, Jürgen (2005) Religion in the Public Sphere. Holberg Prize Lecture, Bergen 2005. <www.holbergprisen.no/images/materiell/2005_symposium_habermas.pdf>

Habermas, Jürgen and Kalleberg, Ragnvald (1999) *Kraften i de bedre argumenter*. Oslo: Ad notam Gyldendal.

Hagee, John (2006) *Jerusalem Countdown. A Warning to the World*. Lake Mary, FL: FrontLine.

Hagen, Carl I. (2007) *Ærlig talt. Memoarer 1944–2007*. Oslo: Cappelen.

Hareide, Dag (2010) 'Den fjerde samtaleformen'. *Morgenbladet*, 24 September.

Hedges, Paul (2008) 'Concerns About the Global Ethic. A Sympathetic Critique and Suggestions for a New Direction'. *Studies in Interreligious Dialogue* 18 (2), 53–68.

— (2010) *Controversies in Interreligious Dialogue and the Theology of Religions*. London: SCM Press.

— (2013) 'Interreligious Studies', in A. Runehov and L. Oviedo (eds) *Encyclopedia of Sciences and Religion*. New York: Springer, pp. 1076–80.

Heelas, Paul (1996) *The New Age Movement. The Celebration of the Self and the Sacralization of Modernity*. Oxford: Blackwell.

Hegel, G. W. F. (1952) *Phänomenologie des Geistes. Sämtliche Werke. Neue kritische Ausgabe*. Hamburg: Verlag von Felix Meiner.

Heyer, Cressida (2012) 'Identity Politics'. *Stanford Encyclopedia of Philosophy*, Spring 2012. <http://plato.stanford.edu/entries/identity-politics/>

Holth, Gunnar and Kallevik, Kjell Arne (2008) *Horisontar. RLE for ungdomstrinnet*. Oslo: Gyldendal.

Horsfjord, Vebjørn (2011) 'Reaching for the Reset Button for Muslim Christian Relations: Recent Developments in the Common Word Process'. *Studies in Interreligious Dialogue* 21 (1), 1–15.

Hunter, James Davison (1987) *Evangelicalism. The Coming Generation*. Chicago and London: Chicago University Press.

Huntington, Samuel P. (1993) 'The Clash of Civilizations?' *Foreign Affairs* 72 (3), 22–49.

— (1996) *The Clash of Civilizations and the Remaking of the World Order*. New York: Simon and Schuster.

Hussein, Mohammed Kamel (1994) *City of Wrong. A Friday in Jerusalem*. Translated by K. Cragg, from *Qarya zalima* [1954]. Oxford: Oneworld.

Hylland Eriksen, Thomas (2009) 'What is Cultural Complexity?' in Ward Blanton, James G. Crossley and Halvor Moxnes (eds) *Jesus Beyond Nationalism. Constructing the Historical Jesus in a Period of Cultural Complexity*. London: Equinox Press, pp. 9–24.

Ibn Warraq (1995) *Why I am not a Muslim*. Amherst, NY: Prometheus Books.

Illman, Ruth (2006) *Ett annorlunda Du. Reflektioner kring religionsdialog*. Göteborg, Stockholm: Makadam.

— (2011) 'Artists in Dialogue: Creative Approaches to Interreligious Encounters'. *Approaching Religion* 1 (1), 59–71.

Ipgrave, Michael (ed.) (2004) *Scriptures in Dialogue: Christians and Muslims Studying the Bible and the Qur'an Together*. London: Church House Publishing.

Jeanrond, Werner (2010) 'Toward an Interreligious Hermeneutics of Love', in Catherine Cornille and Christopher Conway (eds) *Interreligious Hermeneutics*. Eugene, OR: Cascade Books, pp. 44–60.

Jensen, Roger (2008) 'Sekulær fornuft vs. religiøse følelser'. *Minerva* (2), 84–93.

Johnston, Douglas (ed.) (2003) *Faith-based Diplomacy. Trumping Realpolitik*. New York: Oxford University Press.

Johnston, Douglas and Sampson, Cynthia (eds) (1994) *Religion, the Missing Dimension of Statecraft*. New York and Oxford: Oxford University Press.

Juergensmeyer, Mark (2003) *Terror in the Mind of God. The Global Rise of Religious Violence*. Berkeley, Los Angeles, London: University of California Press.

Jørgensen, Jonas Adelin (2008) *Jesus Imandars and Christ Bhaktas. Two Case Studies of Interreligious Hermeneutics and Identity in Global Christianity*. Frankfurt am Main etc.: Peter Lang.

— (2009) 'Theology of Religions as Interreligious Hermeneutics. Presentation and Discussion of a Typological Model for Theology of Religions on the Basis of Two Field Studies of Syncretistic Religious Movements'. *Kerygma und Dogma* 55, 117–40.

Kaymakcan, Recep (2007) 'Curriculum and Textbook Revisions Regarding the Image of the "Religious Other" in Turkish Religious Education', in *Teaching for Tolerance in Muslim Majority Societies*. Istanbul: Centre for Values Education, pp. 15–33.

Kaymakcan, Recep and Leirvik, Oddbjørn (eds) (2007) *Teaching for Tolerance in Muslim Majority Societies*. Istanbul: Centre for Values Education.

Kelly, Andrew (2004) 'Reciprocity and the Height of God. A Defense of Buber Against Levinas', in Peter Atterton, Matthew Calarco and Maurice Friedman (eds)

Levinas and Buber. Dialogue and Difference. Pittsburgh, PA: Duquesne University Press, pp. 226–32.

Khalid, K. M. (1963) *Ma'a al-damîr al-'insani fi masirihi wa-masirihi*. Cairo: Maktabat al-angilu al-misriyya.

— (1986) *Ma'an 'ala l-tariq. Muhammad wa-l-Masih*. First edition: 1958. Cairo: Dar Thabit.

King, Ursula (1998) 'Feminism: The Missing Dimension in the Dialogue of Religions', in John May (ed.) *Pluralism and the Religions: The Theological and Political Dimensions*. London: Cassell Academic, pp. 40–55.

— (1999) *The World's Scriptures: Resources for Dialogue and Renewal*. Calgary, AB: Department of Religious Studies, The University of Calgary.

Kirkerådet (2006) 'Skriftforståelse og skriftbruk med særlig henblikk på homofilisaken'. *Uttalelse fra Den norske kirkes lærenemnd i sak reist av Møre biskop*. Oslo: Kirkerådet.

Knitter, Paul F. (1985) *No Other Name? A Critical Survey of Christian Attitudes toward the World Religions*. New York: Orbis Books.

— (1995) *One Earth Many Religions. Multifaith Dialogue and Global Responsibility*. New York: Orbis.

— (2002) *Introducing Theologies of Religions*. New York: Orbis Books.

— (2007) '"My God is bigger than your God!" Time for Another Axial Shift in the History of Religions'. *Studies in Interreligious Dialogue* 17 (1), 100–18.

Koselleck, Reinhart (1985) *Futures Past. On the Semantics of Historical Time*. Cambridge, MA: MIT Press.

Kouchok, Kawsar H. (2007) 'How to Teach and Not to Teach Tolerance to Young Children: Some Reflections from the Egyptian Context', in Recep Kaymakcan and Oddbjørn Leirvik (eds) *Teaching for Tolerance in Muslim Majority Societies*. Istanbul: Centre for Values Education, pp. 149–62.

Krämer, Gudrun (2006) 'Anti-semitism in the Muslim World. A Critical Review'. *Die Welt des Islams* 46 (3), 243–76.

Küng, Hans (2008) 'Global Politics and Global Ethic: A New Paradigm of International Relations', in Sturla J. Stålsett (ed.) *Religion in a Globalised Age: Transfers and Transformations, Integration and Resistance*. Oslo: Novus Press, pp. 171–80.

Küng, Hans (ed.) (1995) *Yes to a Global Ethic*. London: SCM Press.

Leirvik, Oddbjørn (1990) *Møte med islam*. Oslo: Pax.

— (1996) *Religionsdialog på norsk*. Oslo: Pax.

— (1999) 'Islamske tekstar. Om Koranen som heilagtekst og skulebok'. <http://folk.uio.no/leirvik/tekster/islamsketekstar.html>

— (2001) *Religionsdialog på norsk. Ny og utvida utgåve*. Oslo: Pax.

— (2002) *Islamsk etikk. Ei idéhistorie*. Oslo: Universitetsforlaget.

— (2004a) 'Religious Education, Communal Identity and National Politics in the Muslim World'. *British Journal of Religious Education* 26 (3), 223–36.

— (2004b) 'Interfaith Dialogue and Liberation Theology: Between Liberal Multiculturalism and Inter-Religious Activism', in Sturla Stålsett and Oddbjørn Leirvik (eds), with Peter Beyer: *The Power of Faiths in Global Politics*. Oslo: Novus, pp. 165–70.

— (2006a) *Human Conscience and Muslim-Christian Relations. Modern Egyptian Thinkers on al-damir*. London: Routledge.

— (2006b) 'Kva var karikatursaka eit bilete på?' *Kirke og Kultur* 111 (2), 147–60.

— (2006c) *Islam og kristendom. Konflikt eller dialog?* Oslo: Pax.

— (2006d) 'Charismatic Mission, Miracles and Faith-Based Diplomacy. The Case of Aril Edvardsen', in Sturla J. Stålsett (ed.) *Spirits of Globalization: The Growth of Pentecostalism and Experiential Spiritualities in a Global Age*. London: SCM Press 2006, pp. 131–44.

— (2010a) *Images of Jesus Christ in Islam*. London and New York: Continuum.

— (2010b) '*Aw qala: "Li-jarihi"*. Some Observations on Brotherhood and Neighborly Love in Islamic Tradition'. *Islam and Christian-Muslim Relations* 21 (4), 357–72.

— (2011a) 'Antijudaisme i brytning med toleranse i islamsk tradisjon'. *Kirke og Kultur* 116 (1), 29–41.

— (2011b) 'Philosophies of Interreligious Dialogue: Practice in Search of Theory'. *Approaching Religion* 1 (1), 6–24.

— (2011c) 'The Cartoon Controversy in Norway: The New Christian Right and Liberal Fundamentalism Confronting Islam?' in Ulrika Mårtensson et al. (eds) *Fundamentalism in the Modern World, Volume 2: Culture, Media and the Public Sphere*. London: I.B. Tauris, pp. 125–46.

— (2012) 'Alliansebygging, maktkamp og dialog mellom religiøse leiarar', in Cora Alexa Døving and Berit Thorbjørnsrud (eds) *Religiøse ledere. Makt og avmakt i norske trossamfunn*. Oslo: Universitetsforlaget, pp. 216–28.

Lemke, Thomas (2002) 'Foucault, Governmentality, and Critique'. *Rethinking Marxism* 4 (3), 49–64.

Levinas, Emmanuel (1993) *Den annens humanisme. Oversatt og med innledning, noter og et essay av Asbjørn Aarnes*. Oslo: Aschehoug.

— (1998) *Of God who Comes to Mind*. Translated by B. Bergo. Stanford, CA: Stanford University Press.

— (1999) *Alterity and Transcendence*. Translated by M. B. Smith. New York: Columbia University Press.

Lindholm, Tore (1992) 'Article 1. A New Beginning', in Asbjørn Eide et al. (eds) *The Universal Declaration of Human Rights: A Commentary*. Oslo: Scandinavian University Press.

Maalouf, Amin (2000) *In the Name of Identity: Violence and the Need to Belong*. New York: Arcade Publishing.

Mahfouz, Naguib (1988) 'Jannat al-atfâl', in *Khammarât al-qitt al-aswad*. First published in 1969. Cairo: Maktabat Misr, pp. 79–89.

Manji, Irshad (2003) *The Trouble with Islam. A Wake-up Call for Honesty and Change*. Toronto: Random House Canada.

Miskawayh, Ahmad ibn-Muhammad (1968) *The Refinement of Character*. Beirut: The American University of Beirut.

Moosa, Ebrahim (2002) 'The Debts and Burdens of Critical Islam', in Omid Safi (ed.) *Progressive Muslims on Justice, Gender, and Pluralism*. Oxford: Oneworld.

Moxnes, Halvor (1999) 'Trenger Bibelen moralsk kritikk?' in T. B. Pettersen and S. E. Horjen (eds) *Over alle grenser. Festskrift vedNorges Kristelige Studentforbunds 100 årsjubileum*. Oslo: Verbum forlag/Norges Kristelige Studentforbund.

Murad, Abdul-Hakim (n.d.) 'Book Review of Farid Esack's Qur'an, Liberation and Pluralism Oxford: Oneworld, 1997'. <www.masud.co.uk/ISLAM/ahm/esack.htm>

Mæland, Bård (2003) *Rewarding Encounters. Islam and the Comparative Theologies of Kenneth Cragg and Wilfred Cantwell Smith*. London: Melisende.

Najjab, N. (2005) 'Knowing Thy Neighbour?' *This Week in Palestine* 83 (March), 25.

Nehring, Andreas (2011) 'On the Communication of Sacred Texts. Intercultural Comparison or Intercultural Encounter', in David Cheetham, Ulrich Winkler, Oddbjørn Leirvik and Judith Gruber (eds) *Interreligious Hermeneutics. Between Texts and People*. Amsterdam, NY: Rodopi, pp. 381–96.

Newman, J. (1982) *Foundations of Religious Tolerance*. Toronto: University of Toronto Press.

NOU (1995) *Identitet og dialog*. Norges offentlige utredninger 1995: 9. Oslo: Kirke-, Utdannings- og Forskningsdepartementet.

— (2013) *Det livssynsåpne samfunn. En helhetlig tros- og livssynspolitikk*. Norges offentlige utredninger 2013: 1. Oslo: Kulturdepartementet.

Pink, J. (2003) 'Nationalism, Religion and the Muslim-Christian Relationship. Teaching Ethics and Values in Egyptian Schools'. <www.cesnur.org/2003/vil2003_pink.htm>

Plesner, Ingvill Thorson (ed.) (2004) *Stories on Tolerance*. Oslo: The Oslo Coalition on Freedom of Religion or Belief.

Prior, Michael (1997) *The Bible and Colonialism: A Moral Critique*. Sheffield: Sheffield Academic Press.

— (2002) 'Ethnic Cleansing and the Bible'. *Holy Land Studies* 1 (1), 37–59.

Race, Alan (1983) *Christians and Religious Pluralism. Patterns in the Christian Theology of Religions*. London: SCM Press.

Räisänen, Heikki (1997) *Marcion, Muhammad and the Mahatma*. London: SCM Press.

— (2000) 'På väg mot en etisk bibelkritik'. *Svensk Exegetisk Årsbok* 65, 227–42.

Ramadan, Tariq (2009) 'A Call for a Moratorium on Corporeal Punishment - The Debate in Review', in Kari Vogt, Lena Larsen and Christian Moe (eds) *New Directions in Islamic Thought. Exploring Reform and Muslim Tradition*. London: I.B. Tauris.

Rana, Mohammed Usman (2008) 'Den sekulære ekstremismen'. *Aftenposten*, 25 February.

Rasmussen, Tarald and Thomassen, Einar (eds) (1999) *Kildesamling til Kristendomskunnskap med religions- og livssynsorientering. Vol. 1: Kristendommen. Islam*. Oslo: Nasjonalt Læremiddelsenter.

Rawls, John (1997) 'The Idea of Public Reasoning Revisited'. *The University of Chicago Law Review* 64 (3), 765–807.

— (1999) *A Theory of Justice*. Cambridge, MA: Harvard University Press.

— (2005) *Political Liberalism*. New York: Columbia University Press.

Reiss, Wolfram (2003) 'Die Juden im islamischen Religionsunterricht. Ein Vergleich ägyptischer, jordanischer und palästinensischer Schulbücher. Teil 1: Die Darstellung des Judentums in Ägypten'. *Ökumenische Informationen der katholischen Nachrichten-Agentur* 49, 8–15.

Ricoeur, Paul (1994) *Oneself as Another*. Chicago: University of Chicago Press.

Roald, Anne Sofie (1998) 'Feminist Reinterpretation of Islamic Sources: Muslim Feminist Theology in the Light of the Christian Tradition of Feminist Thought', in *Women and Islamization. Contemporary Dimensions of Discourse on Gender Relations*. Oxford and New York: Berg Publications.

— (2002) 'Religionsdialogiska perspektiv. En fallstudie av en dialoggrupp i södra Sverige', in M. Stenmark and D. Westerlund (eds) *Polemik eller dialog? Nutida religionsteologiska perspektiv bland kristna och muslimer*. Nora: Nya Doxa.

— (2011) 'European Islamic Gender Discourses', in David Cheetham, Ulrich Winkler, Oddbjørn Leirvik and Judith Gruber (eds) *Interreligious Hermeneutics. Between Texts and People*. Amsterdam, New York: Rodopi, pp. 267–88.

Russell, Bertrand (1967) *Why I am Not a Christian and Other Essays on Religion and Related Subjects*. London: Unwin Books.

Said, Edward (2003) *Orientalism*. First edition: 1978. London: Penguin Books.

Salomonsen, Jone (2013) 'Kristendom, paganisme og kvinnefiendskap', in Anders Jupskås Ravik (ed.) *Akademiske perspektiver på 22.juli*. Oslo: Akademika, pp. 73–92.

Schepelern Johansen, Birgitte (2006) 'Islam at the European Universities. Report II'. Copenhagen: University of Copenhagen.

Schirrmacher, Christine (1992) *Mit den Waffen des Gegners. Christlich-muslimische Kontroversen im 19. und 20. Jahrhundert dargestellt am Beispiel der Auseinandersetzung um Karl Gottlieb Pfanders 'Mîzân al-haqq' und Rahmatullâh ibn Khalîl al-'Uthmânî al-Kairânawîs 'Izhâr al-haqq' und der Diskussion über das Barnabasevangelium*. Berlin: Klaus Schwarz Verlag.

Schmid, Hansjörg, Renz, Andreas and Ucar, Bülent (eds) (2010) *'Nähe is dir das Wort . . .' Schriftauslegung in Christentum and Islam*. Regensburg: Verlag Friedrich Pustet.

Schumann, Olaf (1988), *Der Christus der Muslime. Christologische Aspekte in der arabisch- islamischen Literatur*. Köln/Wien: Böhlau Verlag.

Selbekk, Vebjørn (2006) *Truet av islamister*. Oslo: Genesis.

Sirry, Mun'im (2009) '"Compete with One Another in Good Works": Exegesis of Qur'an Verse 5: 48 and Contemporary Muslim Discourses on Religious Pluralism'. *Islam and Christian-Muslim Relations* 20 (4), 423–38.

Skjervheim, Hans (1996) *Deltakar og tilskodar og andre essays*. Oslo: Aschehoug.

Smith, Jane Idleman (2007) *Muslims, Christians, and the Challenge of Interfaith Dialogue*. New York etc.: Oxford University Press.

Smith, Jonathan Z. (2004) *Relating Religion. Essays in the Study of Religion*. Chicago and London: University of Chicago Press.

Smith, Wilfred Cantwell (1978) *The Meaning and End of Religion*. London: S.P.C.K.

Stenström, Hanna (2001) 'En bit till på väg mot en etisk bibelkritik'. *Svensk Exegetisk Årsbok* 66, 177–96.

— (2002) 'Grandma, Räisänen, and the Global Village: A Feminist Approach to Ethical Criticism', in by I. Dunderberg, C. Tuckett and K. Syreeni (eds) *Fair Play. Pluralism and Conflict in Early Christianity. Essays in Honour of Heikki Räisänen*. Leiden: Brill.

Stenström, Hanna (ed.) (2009) *Att tolka Biblen och Koranen. Konflikt och förhandling*. Lund: Studentlitteratur.

Stjernø, Steinar (2005) *Solidarity in Europe. The History of an Idea*. Cambridge: Cambridge University Press.

Strandhagen, Inger J. (2008) 'Unge sjiamuslimer i Oslo. Om religiøs identitet, individualisering og forholdet til transnasjonal autoritet'. Master thesis in Religion and Society, Faculty of Theology, University of Oslo.

Taylor, Charles (2007) *A Secular Age*. Cambridge, MA, and London: The Belknap Press of Harvard University Press.

Tracy, David (1996) 'The Hidden God: The Divine Other of Liberation'. *Cross Currents* 46 (1), 5–16.

Wadud, Amina (2006) *Inside the Gender Jihad: Women's Reform in Islam*. Oxford: Oneworld.

Watt, William Montgomery (1991) *Muslim-Christian Encounters. Perceptions and Misperceptions*. London: Routledge.

Westerlund, David (2003) 'Ahmed Deedat's Theology of Religion: Apologetics Through Polemics'. *Journal of Religion in Africa* 33 (3), 263–78.

Williams, Rowan (2008) 'A Common Word for the Common Good'. <http://rowanwilliams.archbishopofcanterbury.org/articles.php/1107/a-common-word-for-the-common-good>

Wilson, Andrew (ed.) (1991) *World Scripture. A Comparative Anthology of Sacred Texts*. New York: Paragon House/International Religious Foundation.

Winter, Tim (1999) 'The Last Trump Card. Islam and the Supersession of Other Faiths'. *Studies in Interreligious Dialogue* 9 (2), 133–55.

Zebiri, Kate (1997) *Muslims and Christians Face to Face*. Oxford: Oneworld.

Index